THE JET

"Benny 'The Jet' Urquidez—the greatest in more ways than one. A Champion in and out of the ring. The leader of all pioneers. The International lynch pin to all continents. The gentle-spirited humanitarian—my brother."

—Blinky Rodriquez

"I remember Benny coming to me as a kid to train for the first time. He was a hard worker and excelled in everything, which is why he became a champion. His inspiration is why I am still teaching. Mahalo and Aloha from your Sensei Grand Master Hawaiian Kenpo and Kajukenbo."

—Bill Mutsuto Ryusaki

"Benny Urquidez is one of the finest martial artists I've worked with. Because of our efforts, we brought out the best in each other in our memorable fight scenes in *Wheels on Meals*. I hope his book is a huge success."

—Jackie Chan

"The Urquidez contribution to the world of martial arts is inestimable. MMA fighters today should be very thankful they don't have to deal with Benny. Get ready for a walloping good story…"

—David Lee Roth

"Benny Urquidez is the nicest guy you will ever meet—humble to a fault, honest, open, caring, talented, highly skilled, a great teacher and communicator. I'm proud to be his friend."

—Mike Stone

"One of the most remarkable and loving people I have ever met—an inspiration to everyone he touches."

—*John Cusack*

"Ukidokan taught me to be a husband, father, friend, and protector. I dealt with fears that had driven me to dark and scary places. I grew up in the dojo where, under the watchful eye of Sensei Benny Urquidez, I became a man, at last. Sensei has the ability to heal, teach, counsel, and advise in veritably any subject or circumstance."

—*Duff McKagan, Guns N' Roses*

"Benny Urquidez: A Gentleman, a Gentle Man, and the fiercest competitor I've ever had the pleasure to watch in combat. He is an inspiration to all who don a gi."

—*Senior Grand Master Chuck Sullivan, IKCA Kenpo*

"The easiest way to describe my admiration and respect would be to say that I would hope to emulate Benny 'The Jet' in every way as a champion. He is a true warrior, martial artist, and teacher. I treasure every moment with Benny."

—*Don "The Dragon" Wilson*

"Benny 'The Jet' is one of the most unique kickboxers in the world, and one of my favorites to watch because he is relaxed when he fights. Benny is a good, kind man, who is always there to help. Being one who chooses my friends carefully, I am proud to say that Benny has been a close friend for many years."

—*Gokor Chivichyan, 6X World MMA Champion*

"Sensei Ben has been my role model ever since I first met him because he talks the talk and walks the walk. Sensei Benny has shown me what it is to be a Martial Arts Warrior, not just on the mat, but in life, epitomizing the ancient warrior code of Bushido in everything he does."

—*Richard Norton*

THE JET

UKIDOKAN...

U   represents the family Urquidez.

KI   represents the spirit or natural power.

DO   is the Way of the path. It denotes a discipline and philosophy with moral and spiritual connotations, the ultimate aim being enlightenment and personal development. A practitioner of the Way is known as a "master of Strategy."

KAN respresents the house, the house of Urquidez

UKIDOKAN!

THE JET

Sensei Benny Urquidez

with Tom Bleecker

Foreword by Gene LeBell

Gilderoy Publications
Menifee, California

Gilderoy Publications titles are available at quantity discounts for sales promotions, premiums or fundraising. For information, contact Gilderoy Publications, Post Office Box 630, Menifee, CA 92586.

The author of this book does not dispense medical advice or prescribe the use of any technique as a form of treatment for physical or medical problems without the advice of a physician, either directly or indirectly. The intent of the author is only to offer information of a general nature to help you in your quest for emotional and spiritual well-being. In the event you use any of the information in this book for yourself, which is your constitutional right, the author and the publisher assume no responsibility for your actions.

Library of Congress Cataloging-in-Publication Data

Urquidez, Benny 1952-
The Jet / Benny Urquidez with Tom Bleecker / Foreword by Gene LeBell
p.cm.
ISBN 978-0-9653132-3-0 (tradepaper)
Urquidez, Benny 1952- 2. Martial artists—Kickboxing—biography. I. Bleecker, Tom. II. Title.

1st printing, February 2014

The paper used in this publication meets the minimum requirements of the American National Standard for Information Sciences—Performance of Paper for Printed Library Materials, ANSI Z39.48-1984. Printed in the United States of America

Book design by: Kurt Wahlner, www.wahlner.com
Photo restorations by Minh T. Luong

To my mother Lupe,
my sister Lilly,
and my wife Sara—
the three great pillars
throughout my life.
Lilly groomed me for
life itself from the time
I was ten years old.
My mother was my protector.
Sara is my challenger.

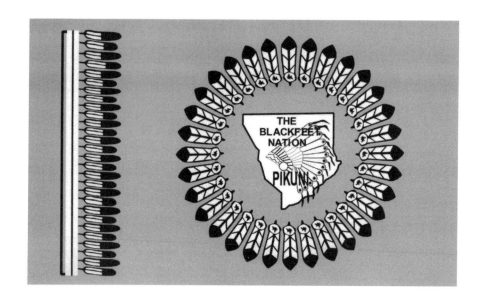

A multitude of single eagle feathers create a circle. Inside the circle is the current land base of the Blackfoot Nation. To the left of the circle of feathers stands the traditional flag of our people—the Eagle Feather staff.

Colors and design represent the Earth, the cosmos, the elements, the plants and the animal, as well as the people.

The circle represents the cycle of life, people are connected, always were, always will be, the circle never ends. The many feathers equate the many bands of the proud and numerous Blackfoot arranged in a circle, beginning in a clockwise direction, as life is. The sun rises in the East, circles to the West, the moon rises and sets in this circular motion, as is the cosmos. Blackfoot people pitch our lodges with the doors to the East, knowing that we start life with the circle in mind, it is perpetual.

Feathers represent the majestic and mysticism of the Eagle. Eagle feathers represent long life, energy, power, and accomplishment. The way the eagle feathers are arranged on the side traditional staff represent the buffalo boss ribs. Buffalo is the staff of life to the Blackfoot.

Contents

▼ ▼ ▼ ▼

Thundering Iron Horse

Foreword

▼ ▼ ▼ ▼

It scems that I've known the Urquidez family forever. Beginning in the mid-1960s, there were several prominent fighting
families, but none stood out like the Urquidez Clan. Anyone
who participated in noncontact tournament fighting, particularly
Ed Parker's Long Beach Internationals, knew that when the Urquidez brothers walked into the Sports Arena with their gis slung
over their shoulders, it was going to be a real rock 'em, sock 'em
weekend.

I first met Benny when he was an adolescent kid. He had a
warm smile and a cute, boyish face. What many mistook as shy-
ness was actually a display of respect that he had for his teachers
and elders. Throughout all the many years that I've known Benny,
I never once heard him cuss or have a bad word to say about anyone, which are a tribute to the love and admiration he has carried
throughout his life for his devoted and caring mother, Lupe.

Although Benny excelled in all aspects of the martial arts,
he'll always be remembered as the greatest pound-for-pound
kickboxer of all time. From his first professional fight, he had

all the ingredients of a champion—he was fearless, knowledgeable, determined, could take a punch, and possessed an arsenal of devastating weapons. Most of all, he had the mindset of a true warrior, much of which I suspect came from his Native American ancestry. In the ring he was a fierce and relentless pit bull who gave new meaning to the old saying, "It's not the size of the dog in the fight that counts, but the size of the fight in the dog." Once Benny took out his axe and went after an opponent, the curtain had begun to drop. What mesmerized and thrilled his legions of worldwide fans is that Benny defeated his opponents with such grace and style. In the ring, he was both a devastating fighter, yet at the same time was entertaining. Without question, everyone who has ever attended a Benny "The Jet" fight came away knowing that they got more than their money's worth.

Both inside and outside the ring, Benny was always a gentleman. If an opponent landed a good shot, Benny would step back and acknowledge his opponent with a smile and a nod. He wasn't mocking his opponent, he was being sincere. Many don't know this about Benny, but after every fight, he offered to take his opponent to dinner for the sole purpose of sharing with that fighter how they could improve their skills and overall fight game. Also, the ritual of touching gloves at the start of the first round was initiated by Benny, who never fought out of anger, but fought for the love of the sport and his desire to continually improve.

What impressed me most about Benny was that his belief in himself was so strong that he was willing to take chances that other fighters were unwilling to take. When a fighter begins their professional career, they must be careful how they pick their opponents. Lose too many matches early on or get knocked out in the opening rounds, and your career is over. This is much like the film industry. An actor, director, or producer's first few films will make or break them. Benny didn't care. From his first fight to his last, he had a standing, open challenge that he would fight anyone, anywhere, and under their rules. He feared no one, ducked no one, and took on all comers—which is the sign of a true champion.

This is one of many reasons why throughout his stellar career Benny had such a huge worldwide following and why promoters in all countries knew that they couldn't lose money promoting a Benny "The Jet" Urquidez fight.

It's difficult to imagine where the sport of kickboxing would be today had it not been for the pioneering and tireless work of Benny Urquidez over the past four decades. Besides establishing himself as a legend and martial arts icon, his tireless efforts resulted in opening doors for many other kickboxers, both here in the US as well as internationally. Not surprisingly, many of the champions who went on to greatness were trained by Benny.

It's been my experience that the majority of people who take up the marital arts do so for one reason—to learn self-defense. While that's a good reason, most people don't stay around long enough to find out that there is so much more to be gained from studying the martial arts than learning how to kick and punch and escape a lapel grab. Benny stands out as a martial artist who recognized the bigger picture early in his training. Because of this, his art is far more than a means of self-defense. To Benny, his personal art that he founded—Ukidokan—is a way of life. Due to his vast experience in many fields both inside and outside the martial arts, Benny has become a great teacher who has dramatically changed the lives for the better of countless numbers of his students.

Over the past more than six decades, the martial arts in the US, as well as abroad, has grown tremendously and is now studied by millions of people. Unfortunately, our martial arts community in America has fewer leaders today than it ever has. Benny is one of those few leaders. He has become a true spiritual warrior. Back in the days of the samurai during Feudal Japan, the young samurai were warriors who fought and died on the battlefields and lived by the honor Code of Bushido. In later years, however, many surviving samurai became spiritual (peaceful) warriors, and every breath they took was Bushido. Another term used historically for this small minority of surviving samurai warriors was "sword saints." In my opinion, Benny is one of the few surviving warriors from decades past who have in their personal living become a sword saint.

Benny has worked hard all his life. In fact, I know few people inside and outside the martial arts who have worked as hard and as consistently as Benny Urquidez. In addition to his hard work ethic, he has remained married for more than 40 years. Having been raised in Southern California and spent much of his adult years in the Hollywood film industry, keeping a marriage intact for more than four decades is a rarity. Besides being a loving husband, he is also a loving father, grandfather, and has a countless number of close personal friendships that have lasted for many decades.

I am delighted that Benny's life story is being written. I think it's long overdue. As you read through these pages, you'll no doubt be impressed by both the high points and low points of this true warrior. His openness about his entire life experience is truly refreshing and took great courage. As you will read, Benny has not led an easy life. He has sacrificed much to obtain the rich and fulfilling life that he and his family enjoy today. Most important, his many achievements have been the result of a life lived with honor and integrity.

Even though Benny is unofficially retired from the ring, even at over 60 years of age, he could still fight with the best. I very much look forward to seeing what accomplishments Benny will achieve in the future. Personally, knowing him as I have for all these years, I believe that he's just warming up and that the best is still yet to come. Should you run into Benny "The Jet" anywhere in his worldwide travels, take a moment to shake his hand and thank him for making this world a better place and for enriching the lives of so many. In his day, he was the best fighter in the world, and now he is content with being the best teacher in the world.

GENE LeBELL

ONE

Childhood

▼　▼　▼　▼

O n June 20, 1952, Long Island Railroad's engineers went
on strike, stranding thousands New York's angry com-
muters, the White Sox defeated the Yankees at Comis-
key Park, Harry S. Truman was President of the United States,
the raging Korean War was at a stalemate, Jersey Joe Walcott was
boxing's heavyweight champion of the world, Al Martino's "Here
in my Heart" was the Number One song—and I was born in a
Southern California hospital to Arnold and Guadalupe Urquidez

Decades earlier, my parents were raised in a natural athletic
environment passed on through generations of their Spanish and
Native American Apache ancestry (although my blood lineage is
Apache, in later years I was adopted into the Blackfoot Nation).

My mother, a beautiful woman with a radiant smile, was
strong physically and mentally. In the 1940s, she performed as
a professional wrestler known as Crazy Linda at the Olympic
Auditorium that was located in downtown Los Angeles. Built in
1924, it was the largest indoor venue in the United States and sat
15,300 spectators. Throughout the 1930s, 1940s, and 1950s the

My mother Guadalupe and father Arnold Urquidez (My brother Arnold is sitting on my mother's lap, my sister Alexis "Eva" is sitting on my father's lap)

"Benito" age five

My mother Guadalupe Urquidez
in her early 20s

Olympic Auditorium was home to some of the biggest boxing, wrestling, and roller derby events.

When I was a child, my mom would take me to watch her wrestle, and it was brutal. She often had welts and a bald spot on her head, but she would tell me not to worry, that the sport of wrestling was fake and her opponents weren't really hitting her. It didn't matter if I believed her because it was clear to me at an early age that she feared no one.

My father was a professional boxer and was a regular at the Olympic Auditorium. He was a good boxer whose dream was to become a great boxer. Because of him, while other kids grew up with fire trucks and teddy bears, I grew up with boxing gloves. When I was three years old, my father began training me. When I turned five, he would tell my brother and me to put on our boxing gloves and take off our shoes, and we would box in a vacant field that was filled with wood splinters and sharp thorns. As a result, our feet became calloused and tough as leather.

During the late 1950s at the Olympic Auditorium many of

The famed Olympic Auditorium in the early 1950s

the trainers' sons would be trained by their fathers, and we would compete against each other. My dad would show off my younger brother and me because he wanted to show the other trainers how tough we were. It wasn't enough to win the match. My father wanted me to hurt these kids and make them cry. To him, the way to succeed in life was controlling people through fear and intimidation. At the same time, he drilled it into me that no one would ever intimidate and instill fear in me—in my world, fear didn't exist and never would.

When I began fighting against these other kids, I was angry at my dad. Besides the painful training in that field of splinters and thorns, he never asked me whether or not I wanted to box, and if I didn't win, he would hit me with a clothes hanger or his belt. No matter how hard or for how long he hit me, I never cried. While this frustrated him, I felt that this made him proud because he took my not crying as a sign of strength. I beat those kids not because I feared my dad, but because I wanted him to be proud of me and show him that I was as tough as he was.

While the other trainers gave their kids small, cheap medals as incentives, our prize from my dad was a donut from the Helm's man who drove a bakery truck filled with freshly baked bread, cakes, and donuts. This was my inspiration, and I would hurt those kids fast just to get that donut. Even at a young age I was a big spender. While my brother always asked for the five-cent chocolate or powdered donut, I found a way to score the six-cent jelly donut for an extra penny.

Although my father was very physical, and often violent, he could also be charming, especially to the ladies. He was a classy dresser who wore a shiny zoot suit, hat, chain that led to his vest pocket and gold pocket watch, and a splash of his favorite cologne. Back in the 1950s, dance halls were popular in the big cities, and he was a regular patron. He was a great dancer, so much so that many of the young ladies mingled around him—sometimes paraded in front of him—hoping he would ask them to dance. My dad was the epitome of "hip, slick, and cool." Throughout my childhood, he was bigger than life.

The Helms Man brings my donuts!

Star "lefty" pitcher for the Giants, which is how I felt.

My family lived on Alpine Street in an area of downtown Los Angeles called Bunker Hill. We occupied a two-bedroom apartment that was the upper residence of a stucco duplex. My sisters Eva, Linda, Delores, and Lilly were in one bedroom, my parents were in the other bedroom, and my brothers Arnold, Adam, Ruben, and I slept in the living room. Even though the nine of us were crammed like sardines into this tiny apartment, we were happy and content with what little we had.

Ours was a busy and noisy household. As kids, we found simple ways to amuse ourselves. The living room black and white 3-knob TV was often on, as was the radio or my dad's RCA Victor record player (although the smaller 45 rpm records were just coming in with Rock 'n' Roll, my father had a prize collection of 78 rpm vinyl records). My sisters would help my mom with the cooking and doing the laundry. As a family we didn't regularly attend church, except for Catholic mass on Christmas Eve and Easter Sunday, although I couldn't understand one word of either service. Throughout her life, the evidence of my mother's religion was reflected in her lifestyle.

I'm fortunate to have spent my childhood growing up in the 1950s and 1960s when as a society we went from AM radio to the Moon. It was a more pleasant, simpler time when everyone said good morning to their neighbor. I can still recall my mom standing on the porch yelling for me to come home, hot summer nights with all the windows open because we didn't have air conditioning, running through the sprinklers, Saturday morning cartoons, jumping on the bed and pillow fights, and drinking water from a hose. The Fifties were a time when a kid got tired from just playing, when a quarter was a fair allowance, when water balloons were the ultimate weapon, and when ANY parent could discipline ANY kid, or feed him, or use him to carry groceries.

Although my father was tough on me and my brothers, my mom knew that we were strong enough to handle anything he did to us. When it came to my father being rough with my sisters, however, my mother made it clear to my dad that they were off

My mother standing outside our apartment in the Pacoima projects, 1958

limits. Then one day, he hit my sister Lilly in her face with his fist. My mom saw it and told my dad that if he ever hit Lilly like that again, she'd kill him. My father angrily replied that he was the man of the house and that he'd hit Lilly any time he wanted. That was a big mistake. My mom put him in the hospital and the following day took out a restraining order against him. For many years, my siblings and I were forbidden to speak my father's name and nobody asked if anyone had heard from him. I can't say that I missed my father. For years he hadn't been around much, anyway. Even when I was sick, he never came to me and felt my forehead to see if I had a fever or ask how I was feeling. Although as a child I loved and admired him, the harsh reality was that he was a tough man who lacked the ability to display concern and affection for his children.

Although there were times when my mother had to accept government assistance in the form of food subsidies, particularly after my father left, she refused to go on welfare. On the 15th and 30th of each month we ate real eggs, but for the rest of the month we ate powdered eggs and drank powdered milk. On the first of each month, my mom bought a five-pound sack of beans, a five-pound sack of rice, and a ten-pound sack of flour, which would last the entire month. From time to time, we would take the bus to LA's Chinatown to buy produce and, on special occasions, a bag of everyone's favorite almond cookies. To this day, I can close my eyes and instantly recall the smell of my mother's homemade tortillas. Sometimes when Christmas arrived, she was short on money to buy gifts for all us kids. Thankfully, the local churches and store owners would deliver toys and food to low income families. During hard times, my mother's spirit was never down, and she always reminded us that Maker (I use Maker synonymously with God) would provide for us.

Even though we lived in the low income area of Los Angeles, my mother was relieved that at least we weren't living on the Indian reservation where, according to her, we would be considered less than dogs. Soon after we arrived in the city, which my parents referred to as the concrete jungle, my mother insisted that we never talk about our Native American heritage.

From the time I was old enough to talk, my mom nurtured me and said that I had a "special gift" and that I was the one who would carry on our Native American traditions and put the Urquidez name on the map. I'd sit at the kitchen table eating and listening to my sisters agreeing with my mother and have absolutely no idea what they were talking about. Sometimes at night I would lie awake and think about what my mother told me and wonder about the nature of this gift she spoke of. It was true that I felt different from others. While I found this intriguing, there were times when *feeling* different bothered me, and times when *being* different caused problems in my life.

In my father's absence, my mom began working a double shift at a local bakery. My older brother Arnold and my older sister Eva got jobs and helped out with finances. On weekends I'd hit the streets and shine shoes for a quarter. In the beginning I didn't know how to shine shoes and would accidently smear polish on my customers' socks. Regardless, they would give me a tip because I always found a way to make them laugh, often giving them a little show, popping the shoe rag as I laid down a perfect spit-shine. Besides shining shoes, I earned money mowing lawns, running errands, or washing cars. At an early age I was becoming a street hustler and could earn five dollars a week, which in the late 1950s was a whopping amount of money for a kid. In fact, five bucks would buy 86 six-cent jelly donuts from the Helm's man!

Unlike today, in the 1950s and 1960s there weren't gangs in Los Angeles. Instead there were car clubs, and my two oldest brothers, Arnold and Mando, belonged to separate clubs that had chapters in most of the major cities. When we lived on Bunker Hill, my brothers threw parties at night that were fueled by loud music and a parade of cars coming and going. In those days, practically everyone smoked cigarettes and drank alcohol. As an adolescent kid, I was intrigued by it all and would climb onto the roof and watch the unfolding activities, especially the girls.

It was around that time that Arnold began studying karate with Bill Ryusaki, a tall, tough Hawaiian who had a school in North Hollywood. The first time Arnold came home wearing his karate gi, I thought I'd die laughing because to me it looked like he'd been driving around in his pajamas.

Among LA and San Fernando Valley's macho car clubs, fights were common. One night, a rival car club crashed my brothers' party, and one of its members threw gasoline on Arnold and lit him on fire. Arnold ran inside the house, and his friends threw him in the shower and then drove him to the hospital. A half hour later, I watched members of my brothers' car clubs angrily jump in their cars and drive off to extract retribution.

The projects in Pacoima as they are in 2014

When my mom learned about the attack on Arnold, she said it was time to go. Weeks later, we moved to the projects in Pacoima, which were three acres of state housing surrounded by ten foot iron-tipped fences. Around that time, a *Los Angeles Times* staff writer described Pacoima as consisting of "sagging, leaning shacks and backhouses framed by disintegrating fences and clutter of tin cans, old lumber, stripped automobiles, bottles, rusted water heaters, and other bric-a-brac of the back alleys." Moreover, in the late 1950s Pacoima lacked curbs, paved sidewalks, paved streets, and had what the article described as "dusty footpaths and rutted dirt roads that in hard rains become beds for angry streams." When my family moved to Pacoima, three-quarters of its population was of Hispanic/Latino descent. The remaining were African American, as well as immigrants from Mexico, Guatemala, and Salvador.

Not surprisingly, life in the projects was akin to living in a war zone. Crime, drugs, blaring music, fights, domestic violence, and the coming and going of marked and unmarked police cars were everyday occurrences. Because there was little trust in the projects, people were constantly peering from their windows. If someone drove into the projects that no one knew, a system of phone tag would alert everyone that there was an intruder, and the gates would be locked, trapping them inside.

Eventually, Arnold rented a house outside the projects and got married. A month later, my oldest sister Eva couldn't handle living there anymore and left, and was soon followed by my sister Linda. This left my mother, Mando, Lilly, Delores, Ruben, my youngest brother Adam, and myself.

When we lived in Pacoima, I attended Sun Valley Elementary School. From the beginning, I truly wanted to do well so that my mom would be proud. Besides, I looked forward to going to school because it got me away from the projects, and I could be around sane people because most everyone in the projects was crazy.

Because my mother knew that when I began attending elementary school, the teacher and kids would ask about my nationality, she told me to tell them that I'm an American, period. As a child, I was confused because it was clear to me that my mom was proud of her Native American heritage, and yet at the same time she was troubled by what she envisioned as this causing trouble in my life. Whatever the problem was, from an early age, I felt driven to rectify it, although at the time I had no idea how I was going to do this.

Unfortunately, from the start, things didn't go well in school. Whenever I wasn't clear about what the teachers were saying, I'd question them. Because of my straightforward nature that was instilled in me by my father, my teachers felt that I was challenging them. In response, they would hold me up to the class as an example of bad behavior, which, in turn, made me feel stupid and caused me to become angry.

It wasn't long before many of the teachers felt highly intimidated by me. Because of what I'd learned from my older brothers and sisters, as well as a strong fight game that I'd been taught by my father, I was equipped with a fiery attitude. Whenever a teacher would tell me to go to the principal's office, I'd snap back that

I wasn't going. If I was told to stand in the corner, I'd reply that I wasn't doing any such thing. It wasn't long before one of the teachers made the mistake of grabbing me, which resulted in my delivering a crippling body shot to his liver. My father had taught me how and where to hit an opponent. Within a short time, word spread among the teachers to avoid at all cost grabbing me.

I was just as uncontrollable outside the classroom and was often busted for fighting during recess and while walking to and from school. Fights were usually the result of my light skin and blonde hair. Other times, the kids made fun of me for carrying my shoes and walking barefoot to school, which I did because I didn't want to wear them out. From an early age, my shoes and clothes were important to me, which was another part of my personality that I learned from my father.

I was no stranger to the police. My crimes weren't anything serious, but amounted to petty vandalism, shoplifting, and fighting. Shortly after I turned eight, my younger brother ("Mighty Adam") and I stole a car. The problem was that we were both too small to drive, and so he sat on the seat and steered while I laid on the floorboard and worked the pedals with my hands. While steering, Adam would call for gas and I'd give it to him; when he called for brakes, I'd hit the brakes. I don't know what we were thinking, but the plan was doomed from the start. Not long into our joyride, Adam yelled out, "Cops!" and without a thought I jammed the gas pedal to the floor. The car rocketed forward, jumped a curb, and smashed into a wall. Thankfully, neither of us was hurt, although the front of the car was heavily damaged.

An hour later, the cop who responded to the scene of the crash arrived at our house with me and Adam in tow. My mother opened the door, unsurprised to find herself looking at a police officer.

"Lupe, these your kids?" he asked.

"Yes," my mom replied.

He told her about our joyriding and the car wreck. Relieved that no one was hurt, my mother promised to discipline us. After the cop left, she sat us down and explained that what we did was wrong and that there are consequences for poor behavior. Feeling that I had disappointed my mother was far worse than the most severe physical beating I ever received from my father.

Two weeks later, my mother learned that the juvenile authorities, having reviewed the police officer's report of the stolen car incident, planned to put me in juvenile hall. As part of a plea bargain, my mother agreed to move me out of Pacoima, so in 1960 my family moved to Morgan Hill, which is approximately 24 miles south of San Jose and where my mother's brother had a five acre fruit farm. In the early 1960s, the area was home to hundreds of farmers who oversaw highly organized orchards and crops before the entire area became part of the computer empire that was soon known throughout the world as Silicon Valley.

For the better part of a year, my family lived on that farm, which was a sharp contrast to the life we'd left in the projects. In addition to the smell of farm animals and my allergies to pollen, the wind and dust were a constant presence, as was the dull nature of mostly everyone who lived in this rural farm community.

Along with attending school and helping with chores that included picking fruit, my brother Ruben and I joined a local judo school and began taking lessons. Powerfully built, Ruben became an expert judo practitioner. As a footnote, in later years, he became an army sergeant and was like a locomotive in the ring.

As was the case in Pacoima, it wasn't long before I was getting in trouble. About a month after arriving in Morgan Hill, I started going out at night, mainly because I was curious about what people were doing. I'd wander into town and watch people partying and acting stupid. I'd climb trees and observe how guys picked up girls, fascinated by life unfolding before me. From an early age and well into my young adult years, I was drawn to a special time of night that I called the witching hour.

When I'd return home, usually in the wee hours of the morning, I'd often bring "stuff" home with me. I was a coyote. When my mother and uncle would ask where I got these things, which sometimes included money, I'd say I found them. It was around this time that my sister Linda nicknamed me "Pockets." My mom knew I was up to my old tricks, even though she didn't say anything. Finally, my uncle put his foot down and told my mom, "You have to do something about Benito." A few days later, my mother picked up the phone and called my brother Arnold.

TWO

Adolescent and Teen Years

▼　▼　▼　▼

In 1961 when I turned nine, my mom sent me to live with my brother Arnold, who was a real slave driver. I slept on the living room sofa, obediently did chores, and every day upon returning home showed him a slip of paper confirming that I'd attended school.

Arnold was very physical, and by 1961 had earned a black belt in Shotokan karate from Sensei Bill Ryusaki. Convinced that karate lessons would help instill discipline in me, Arnold signed me up without asking if I was interested, which was reminiscent of when my father five years earlier insisted that I fight kids at the Olympic Auditorium. Every day after school I'd hide in the closet or behind the sofa, and Arnold would find me and drag me to karate lessons. Finally, I got so mad with this cat-and-mouse game that I thought *I'm going to train and get so good I'm going to beat him up!*

After a month of taking lessons, although I was learning discipline, I was a handful. I used to body shot these kids, who became terrified of me. They'd cry and run to their parents, who would then tell my brother and Sensei Bill, "Benny's hurting my son. He doesn't belong in the 8 to 10 year old group. He should be with the 12 and 13 year olds. He's hitting too hard."

The truth was that whenever I hit those kids, I heard my father in my head telling me to gain respect by doing as much damage as possible. I was so aggressive that some of the parents thought I was on something because I had so much energy. Besides having been trained this way by my father, I wanted to prove to Sensei Bill that I was tough. He had something more important on his mind, however, and would tell me, "Benny, you have to stop hurting these boys because I need them to pay my rent."

I oozed confidence, and after six months I became a triple threat—judo, boxing, and karate. Unlike the other kids, I wasn't afraid of getting hit and had the warrior heart of a lion. In addition to having grown up in the projects, I'd been hit in the ring at the Olympic Auditorium, was regularly beaten by my father, and had dozens of street fights under my belt. Many of the adults who trained with Bill Ryusaki were so impressed with my skills

With Bill Ryusaki today

ABOVE: Early tournament win as a white belt

Around the time I began karate with Sensei Bill Ryusaki

From the left: My mother, Ruben, "Smiley," and me

that they gave me advice because they wanted to take credit for me. Sensei Bill was also impressed, so much so that he used me and my brothers as teachers because we were excellent fighters. Short on money, my brothers and I cleaned the dojo to pay for our training.

As time passed, I began to get a sense of the gift that my mother told me I arrived with at birth. Besides hearing and seeing things that others didn't hear or see, I knew how things worked (having no prior knowledge of that particular thing), and began to remember things that had never been taught to me. Moreover, people noticed that I was extremely intuitive and began referring to me as an "old soul." When I talked with my mom about this, she said that my gift was from Maker. As much as this gift was a blessing, as my life unfolded, it would prove to be a double-edged sword.

Over the next year that I lived with Arnold, I didn't see my mother, although we talked regularly on the phone. To say that I missed her would be a vast understatement. Then in 1964 around the time I turned 12, my mom, along with my brothers and sisters who had remained in Morgan Hill, moved back to North Holly-wood and rented a house a few blocks from Arnold. I was happy that I'd been reunited with the rest of my family. We were so close that outside people didn't exist. To my mom, her kids were every-thing, which is why she chose never to remarry. Throughout her life, she often spoke of "familia" and that we should only—and always—trust and back up our immediate family members.

After my family's return, because my karate training had taught me discipline, Arnold convinced my mom that I could move back with her. I was ecstatic. It was as if I had gotten back my security blanket. My mother was the only person with whom I ever felt totally safe. I could put my head on her lap, and she would brush my hair with her hand and make everything right.

I've always been a highly emotional person. At times, my emotional reactions to the words and actions of others—as well

Adam, Ruben, my mother, and me at age 14

as my own thoughts—were so intense that when I felt my emotions boiling up inside, I'd repress them. Keenly aware of this, my mother became my nurturer who protected my feelings and my thoughts. In a sense, she was the valve on my emotional pressure cooker.

The house that my mom rented was in disrepair and sat on a lot that included a small one bedroom shack in back. Although our neighbors had beautiful lawns, our house had dirt, and every day my mom would make me rake the dirt to make it look nice. The porch was unsteady and needed paint, there was a hole in the kitchen floor, and the garage actually leaned like the Tower of Pisa.

Delores, Lilly, Adam, Ruben, my mom, Alfred, and I lived in the front house. No one lived fulltime in the back house, although eventually Adam began to sleep there and my sister Linda used it to throw parties.

For years I remembered my father as a true Rico Suave—the Latin lover stereotype with greased hair, gold chains, polished shoes, and flowing shirt—a guy who exudes cool confidence and says, "Hey, girls, take a look at this!" Beginning around the age of ten, I took on that persona and began dressing up far beyond anything the kids my age were doing. I mean I was outlandish.

Coupled with all the grownup information I was getting from my older siblings and the adults at the karate dojo, I was starting to make moves in the world and acquiring physical possessions. Whether it would be a good way or a bad way didn't matter. Although I didn't have an honest paying job, I made money from various shady street hustles. One way or another, I got what I wanted.

Also, while most kids my age were interested in riding their bikes and collecting baseball cards, my main interest was eying the older girls, whom I often saw as challenges. The girls my age didn't interest me because they had undeveloped bodies, acted silly, and talked stupid baby talk. Around the time I turned 12, Lilly, who was four years older, began referring to me as "Little Big Man" and teaching me about girls. In the absence of my father,

Fighting as a brown belt in 1965

she was the one who gave me the talk about the birds and the bees and, for future reference, began schooling me on the type of girls to date and the type to avoid.

I continued to spend much of my time working out at the karate dojo. Besides having greatly improved my fighting skill, I was mastering katas and weapons. Then on August 2, 1964, a major milestone in my martial arts career occurred when, along with my brothers, I attended the biggest karate tournament in the world—the Long Beach Internationals that were promoted by Kenpo black belt Ed Parker and held at the Long Beach Municipal Auditorium. Throughout the day, I sat in awe as I watched adults of all belt ranks compete in the most sensational karate fighting I'd ever witnessed. The final matches and demonstrations were held that evening in the same auditorium where the multi-ring elimination matches had earlier taken place.

Among the demonstrations, Jhoon Rhee, who stood 5'5", gave an incredible display of aerial kicking, shattering pine boards held seven feet in the air. Ben Largusa thrilled the audience with a performance of the Filipino deadly stick-fighting art of escrima. Takyuki Kubota demonstrated what *Black Belt* magazine called "shocking feats," eight-year-old Roy Castro, the son of renowned Bay Area black belt Ralph Castro, gave a demonstration that brought the crowd to its feet with resounding applause, and Bruce Lee wowed and captivated the audience with an amazing, jaw-dropping demonstration that is still talked about to this day.

The hour was well after midnight when I arrived home. At three in the morning, I laid awake in bed, electrified by what I'd witnessed in Long Beach. As I fell off to sleep, I vowed to one day compete in that same tournament, that I would be a devastating force to reckon with, and that I would make my mark.

Throughout my childhood, while my brothers were teaching me to be a warrior, my mother and sisters were teaching me to be self-sufficient. By the time I became a teenager, I knew how to

The late '60s and early '70s the Van Nuys Boulevard scene

With Adam "Smiley" and my mom, early 1970s

cook, market, clean house, and wash and iron my clothes, including how to put pleats in my pants and wire my shirts and socks.

It was around this time that Lilly and I became dance partners, and there wasn't a dance contest anywhere in LA—including the cha-cha, Maringa, swing, or jerk—that we couldn't win. Although I was young looking, because I was mature for my age and came with my sisters, the doormen looked the other way.

During my early teenage years, I attended Pacoima and Sun Valley Junior High Schools. I was one of the most popular kids in school and always had a crowd of people around me. Like my father, I was dressed to kill. I'd arrive at school wearing purple pants, orange suede shoes, purple slacks, shiny knitted see-through shirts, bell bottoms, and a pompadour with a squared-off ducktail. I was great at schmoozing with the girls, and because I was trained in karate and winning tournaments, I had all the guys spooked. My school peers could feel my energy just by my walking past them.

Along with my siblings and their friends, I partied at all hours of the night and into the early morning. In keeping with the time, the back house was adorned with psychedelic and black lights. There was always a party going on. People would just arrive, often with booze and dope. Across the nation, the hippie generation was in full swing. Huge gathering like those in Haight-Ashbury and Woodstock were commonplace, as were protest demonstrations, both violent and nonviolent. There was music everywhere—the Power of Power, Grand Funk Railroad, Chicago Transit Authority, the Carpenters, and The Oldies, among others. This was the Sixties—Dr. Leary's call to "turn on, tune in, and drop out," coupled with Beatle mania, tie-dye, free love, bell bottoms, love beads, and the constant hippie revolution against the Establishment and the escalating Vietnam War. Having lived through this period, I can attest to the validity of the old quip about the Sixties: "If you can remember them, you weren't there."

My mom never visited the back house, even though she knew what was going on. I could feel her energy when she would look

Taken at Arnold's dojo on Chase Street in North Hollywood

Early noncontact tournament fighting as a black belt

through the curtains to make sure that I was with my brothers and sisters. She wouldn't go to sleep until all of us returned to the front house, at which time she cooked us a hot meal before we went to sleep. I made certain that my mother never saw me drunk, smoke, or loaded. I never fought with her because I loved her too much. Not once did she ever hear me cuss or speak negatively about anything. The boundless respect that I had for my mother was how I showed the love I had for her in return for her unconditional love, nurturing, and protection that allowed me to walk through life without fear, to learn from my own mistakes, and to grow.

It was around this time that a young kid named Bill "Blinky" Rodriguez walked into my brother Arnold's dojo with a sincere interest in training. Because Blinky didn't have any money, Arnold gave him a scholarship. Within a short time, Blinky began hanging out at our house on a regular basis and often spent the night. Because he was around my age (two years younger), we became friends and started training together.

When it came to school and academia, I was barely keeping my head above water and spent as much time sitting in the principal's office as I did attending classes and doing my homework. I couldn't wait to the final bell to ring so that I could get over to the dojo and train. After the evening class ended, my brothers and sisters and I would cruise Van Nuys Boulevard, and then later in the evening hit the nightspots where I'd be decked out and styling.

For a while, I hung with the black guys, then the all-Mexican Latin Lads. In time, I joined a car club and drove a pristine, '63 lowered Chevy Impala, and even became part of the Malibu surf crowd and drove a Woody. I was a chameleon and easily fit in everywhere. Of course, my reputation as a deadly martial artist helped fuel my notoriety.

When we weren't partying on weekends, my brothers and I went everywhere to compete in tournaments. Besides local tournaments, we drove to San Francisco, Oakland, and Arizona. The "Urquidez clan," as we became known, wasn't the only family entering tournaments. We often competed against the Alegria and Castalanos families, who were two of the most prominent.

Among my family there was a strong sense of loyalty and an obvious pecking order, with Arnold being our leader and final say with everything pertaining to our martial arts. Our family carried with it a richness and a real wholeness and deep respect, love, and admiration. It was during those many tournaments that I learned discipline, respect for my fellow competitors, and sportsmanship.

My karate training became my main focus, and in 1966, at the age of 14, I broke tradition. In the 1960s a person had to be 18 years of age to be a black belt. This was a time when the martial

With Mr. Ed Parker, a great teacher, mentor, and friend

art was in its infancy in this country. Back then, it was amazing what power the lay public bestowed upon the elite few who wore the black belts. Mysterious, intimidating, at times even cryptic, many of these men were revered as superhumans, if not gods.

Because I was far superior to all the kids and many of the adults who trained at our dojo, American Kenpo founder Ed Parker assembled a panel to test me for black. Overseen by Mr. Parker, Bill Ryusaki, my brother Arnold, Clarence Akuda, Tu'umamao "Tino" Tuiolosega (the founder of Lima Lama), and Tak Kubota, I passed a grueling test that resulted in my being promoted to shodan. After I strapped on my black belt, everyone delivered the ceremonial kick to my midsection and congratulated me, except Arnold, whose kick resulted in a hairline fracture of one of my ribs because he was angry that I'd broken tradition.

A few weeks after I became a black belt, I walked into the Long Beach Sports Arena to enter the 3rd Annual Long Beach Internationals. Months prior, Bruce Lee debuted as Kato on the TV series "The Green Hornet," and because of his amazing kung-fu

Ruben, Mando, myself, and one of my students

moves on that show, the Sports Arena was packed with kids who had begun studying the martial arts. I strutted around, proudly displaying my black belt, thinking, *Look at me. I've got my shodan, my black belt.* I walked over to where the 14-year-olds were gathering and was still posing when one of the officials came up to me and said, "No, no, no, you don't belong here."

I said, "Yeah, I'm fourteen. This is my category. This is my group."

But the man insisted, "No, you're a shodan now. You have to go over there and fight with the other black belts."

I looked over and saw Chuck Norris and Skipper Mullens standing with several dozen black belts and instantly thought, *I can't fight these guys, they're grown men!*

Arnold looked at me and said, "You wanted to be a black belt. That's what you're going to have to deal with."

The first few times I fought as a shodan, I found the smallest adult I could and stood next to him, figuring he wouldn't hurt me too badly. To everyone's surprise, I ended up winning most of my fights, probably because I was running so fast that no one could catch me.

For the next half dozen tournaments, I was the cute kid, and these adult black belts had fun with me and began treating me like their mascot. I was entertaining them, but when I started winning, they began standing next to me on purpose. They wanted to fight me and show me what it was going to take. The rude awakening caused me to be a fast learner. As a footnote, nearly five decades ago, I was the first karateka in the United States to break the tradition of no black belts under the age of 18. Today, children as young as five years old are wearing black belts. In retrospect, Arnold had a point, kicking me for breaking tradition. I didn't understand it then, but I understand it now.

Weeks later, a strange thing occurred that would make no sense until ten years later. Early one morning I walked into the kitchen to find Blinky, who was 13 at that time, sitting at the kitchen table, deep in thought. I put my head down for a long time, and then said, "I don't know how to tell you this, but God has been talking with me." Blinky looked up, suddenly interested, but still silent. "It's true," I continued. "Last night, God told me that you and I were going to travel around the world together." Blinky jumped up and grabbed me. Unbeknownst to me, he had experienced a similar revelation from God an hour earlier and couldn't sleep.

Growing up in the tough part of the San Fernando Valley, I often had to fight my way out of tight fixes. In the company of my brothers and sisters, I roamed Van Nuys and North Holly-wood. When we fought in the street, we didn't believe in leaving the other guy standing because he might come back with a two-by-four and cave in our skulls. We owned the Valley. We'd walk the streets and a dozen kids would follow behind us at a distance. The strong sense of "familia" that my mother instilled in us made me feel secure, particularly because my older brothers and sisters had a reputation of being superb street fighters. There was an unspoken word that if you messed with a Urquidez, the entire Urquidez clan would fall on your head.

We weren't all bad by any means. Our family was aware of the struggles and financial hardships many in our community faced. In an effort to help, throughout the year we gave karate demos at churches, community centers, and the YMCA, as well as helping to promote Cinco de Mayo and participating in fundraisers.

In 1970 at the age of 18, I had my first Harley Davidson. That was one monster motorcycle. I used to stop at a red light, jump off, hold onto the bike, and then when the light changed, I'd jump back on and haul ass.

One afternoon, I was riding my Harley when I noticed a beautiful, tall girl walking across the street and sporting a long mane of black hair that fell to the backs of her knees. She had a well-toned body, which I later learned was the result of her hob-by of Polynesian dancing. Temporarily smitten, I drove over to her and introduced myself. I could tell immediately that she was the quiet, shy type, although she had a friendly, warm smile.

Sara around the time I first met her in 1970

During Sara's modeling career. She could double for Sophia Loren.

She told me her name was Sara Morteo. She was four years younger, had four younger brothers, and came from a well-to-do family. Her father worked as a chef and did catering for some of the finest families, mixed with celebrities, and played percussion as a side job. Later, when I met him, he reminded me of my father because he was a sharp dresser and a great dancer. Sara's mother was a homemaker. Within ten minutes, a spark ignited between Sara and me, and we began seeing more of each other, even though from the beginning she suspected—and probably knew—I was a player.

In the ensuing weeks, I learned of Sara's unique background that was unlike any girl I'd ever met—she is a direct descendent of the leader of the Apache Nation, War Shaman Chief Geronimo. When she was quite young, her family recognized that she had the gift of intuitive vision and the ability to heal. From the beginning, our shared Native American roots brought us together, each of us sensing a specialness in the other, as well as a kinship. The more time I spent with Sara, the stronger I sensed that she was the type of girl that I might get involved with and never get uninvolved. How little did I know at the time how right my intuition was.

Similar to my '63 Chevy Impala, low and slow

THREE

My World
Darkens

▼　▼　▼　▼

It should be of no surprise that in my adult years I was passionately drawn to full contact karate. During my high school years, I wrestled at Poly Technical and played football at North Hollywood. In soccer, when I went to kick the ball, the opposing players would get out of the way because I had powerful legs and sometimes would purposely kick them in the shins. When I played football, the coach would tell me that he needed to "take a player out" and I'd tackle the guy like a freight train and sideline him for the rest of the game. Even my teammates were leery of me. My football coach would say, "Benny, when you practice, can you not hit them so hard?" I'd tell him that the only way I knew to stop someone was to hit them with my full force, and if that hurt them, then maybe they needed to up their weight training.

I truly loved school, especially history and mathematics and learning how things were put together. Unfortunately, it seemed that trouble followed me everywhere I went. I could be one side of the school, and if a fight broke out on the other side of the school, somehow I would be blamed.

As was the case in elementary and junior high school, I'd land in the principal's office and the principal would tell me that everyone was afraid of me. I'd tell the principal I was a nice guy, and he'd say, "You're nice when you want to be, but I've seen your energy and when you want to be mean, you're really one mean person." I'd go on about how much I loved school and that I was willing to sit in the back of the class and say nothing. It didn't matter. I was a major disturbance and had everyone spooked. When I entered high school, that everyone had me pegged as a deadly karate expert didn't work in my favor when it came to mending fences.

When the school bell rang at the end of the day, the party would begin. I'd jump behind the wheel of my lowered Chevy Impala and, along with my friends, cruise Van Nuys Boulevard, eyeing all the girls and hitting Danny's Dogs, the San Fernando Mall, and other hotspots. When I'd grow tired of the Valley scene, I'd park my Impala and drive my Woody to the Santa Monica and Malibu beaches where I'd surf, fight, drink, and party with the tanned bikini-clad beach bunnies.

Ironically, my two lifestyles never crossed paths. No one from the valley ever saw me driving my Woody with my surfboard on top, and no one at the beach ever saw me cruising Van Nuys Boulevard as a low-rider. Regardless of where I drove, I had a big smile on my face, my foot on the gas, and my car stereo blaring whatever music fit the particular scene I was in.

I continued to obtain physical possessions. Cars, motorcycles, a wardrobe fit for a king, and plenty of spending money. Many of these things were given to me by people for no reason other than they wanted to be my friend. I had taken on the persona of my father—Rico Suave—stylish clothes, expensive polished shoes, pompadour, all tied to a line of gab for the girls and an intimidating tone for the guys. Like my father, I regularly danced the night away and was a frequent patron and contestant at the popular El Monte Legion Stadium and 18th Street.

I continued to see Sara. One evening, her family had a party at their home to which I was invited. After I mingled for a while making small talk, I noticed a man staring at me from across the room. I walked over to him and said, "Hi, I'm Benny, Sara's boyfriend." He smiled, told me that he was Sara's Uncle Domingo and that he knew me.

"What?" I asked.

"I know you," he repeated.

"No. If you knew me, I would have recognized you. I don't forget faces."

"Your mother Lupe?"

"Yes, she is."

"You're the one—you and your little brother—stole a car years ago in Pacoima and crashed it into a wall."

What a small world. The man turned out to be the Sheriff of Pacoima who ten years earlier busted me and Adam. Besides being Sara's uncle, he was the person who was grooming her to carry out her family's Native American ways. .

When Sara came to North Hollywood to my family's home with its dirt lawn, rotting front porch, leaning garage, and a kitchen with a hole in the floor, I wasn't embarrassed or ashamed. Not only did I not mind Sara coming to my ramshackle home, I didn't mind if the world showed up at my front door. The reason was that I was so wrapped up in myself that I didn't care what anybody thought of me. And as far as Sara was concerned, had she been bothered by my home, my car, my Rico Suave wardrobe, and/or my self-absorbed rowdy lifestyle, I could always find another girlfriend.

Although I continued with my karate training and fighting in weekend tournaments with my brothers, my real-time fight training was taking place in the street. In the late 1960s, I was a member of The New Generation car club. We were a tough bunch who often got into fights with other car clubs, usually because we were stealing their girls. We fought with chains, bats, and anything else we could get our hands on. By the time I reached my mid-teens, I'd been stabbed twice, shot in the ankle, and on one occasion nearly bled to death from being hacked by a machete. Because of my martial arts training, my car club affiliation, and being a member of the Urquidez clan, I had gained a reputation among the street people that I was a dangerous person to be feared.

During this time when my life was starting to spin out of control, I occasionally got hit with a moment of clarity that would stop me in my tracks. One such incident happened during my senior year at North Hollywood High School where I often harshly demanded that people respect me.

One Friday at lunchtime, I walked up to the school's star football player, who always had a crowd around him that included his pretty girlfriend. Over the course of five minutes, I berated him in front of everyone, trying to get him to fight me. He stood frozen, visibly terrified. I kept ridiculing and humiliating him, called him a coward and a phony with no heart and no guts, and then finally swaggered off, laughing over my shoulder.

When I returned to school the following Monday, I was told that this star football player was looking for me and that he'd brought his father's gun to school. I went looking for him and eventually cornered him in a bathroom. After ordering everyone else out, I walked up to him and said, "I heard you're looking for me. You want to shoot me. So—here I am."

As I walked closer, he started crying. His body shook and his lower lip trembled. "Why did you do this to me?" he said. "Why didn't you just beat me up and put me in the hospital? Why did you have to humiliate me in front of my girlfriend and friends?" He went on that way for another minute. Finally, he couldn't speak. Tears continued falling from his eyes. At the time, I was so hard that I reiterated that he was a pussy and a coward, then challenged him to shoot me in the back as I turned and walked out.

As the morning progressed, for the first time in my life I had a heavy heart. I kept thinking about what I'd done to that guy, and the more I thought about it, the worse I felt. He was right.

I'd done far more damage than had I just beat him up. I had taken away his pride and crippled his spirit.

At lunchtime, I saw him standing with his girlfriend and surrounded by his friends. As I approached, his girlfriend began pleading with me that they didn't want any more trouble. I put my hand up and stopped her. "I'm not here to make trouble," I said. "I'm here to apologize to your boyfriend. What I did last Friday was wrong, and I wasn't honest about him. He's a good man. He's got a strong heart and he's not a coward. You should feel proud to have him as a boyfriend," then I turned to his buddies and told them they should consider themselves fortunate to have him as a friend.

I learned a profound lesson that day. That football player was neither a weakling nor a coward. I knew this because I'd seen him on the football field take many hard hits and never once complained. Far more important, he was able to stand before me and speak honestly from his heart while allowing himself to cry. This was something I knew took great courage. He wasn't doing it out of fear. What he did was something that I couldn't have done. My father had taught me early on that only sissies cry and that crying is the sign of a weak man. I learned that day that my father was wrong about that. I also learned that he was wrong about living a lifestyle that gains respect by instilling fear in people and physically hurting them.

Over the next few days, I wondered about what else my father had taught me that was also wrong. The lesson I learned from this star football player—this moment of clarity—in no way radically changed my life. In the ensuing weeks, I forgot about these revelations, not entirely however, because a seed had been planted.

I continued to find ways to cash in on my fighting and started making side money from backyards fights. People would drive long distances to watch and bet on these fights that were often brutal. I never lost. After a while, my badass reputation became known to local gamblers and loan sharks who began hiring me to collect past due debts for a percentage. I was ruthless, didn't tolerate excuses, and had no problem with inflicting harm on those who didn't pay. Even though I was making money through illegal ventures, I rarely had to spend any of it. I'd walk into a nightclub and never had to pull out my wallet. "Hey, Benny," the owner or doorman would say with a patronizing smile, "We got a place for you." Drinks were on the house or sent over by friends and even people I hardly knew; dope and girls were also on the house. No matter where I went, it was that way.

Aside from my karate workouts and business concerns, I partied around the clock. I would hang at the dance spots in the evening, hit an afterhours clubs or my brother's club The Black Cat until sunrise, go home and sleep for a few hours, shower, then go to Griffith Park and hang out with the hippies playing music and getting loaded or I'd hit the beach and surf until sundown.

Following a couple hours to shower and slip into another Rico Suave outfit, I'd return to the nightclubs and dance spots. I rode my Harley with the motorcycle clubs the Sundowners and the Hell's Angels. Even at that young age, these bikers respected me. Maybe they figured I had legions of demons in me and behind me. I was wild and had no boundaries. On the outside I had become my father—hip, slick, and cool—the ultimate badass Rico Suave—while on the inside I felt ugly.

After living this way for two years, money had no value. Girls had no value. My physical possessions had no value. Worst of all, my life had become that of a man directing people. At times, I felt like God because people were treating me as if I was. Everyone relied on me for everything. Soon their reliance felt demanding and I began to resent it. Was this all there was to my life? Was my life going to be nothing more than one big party with me being the director of energies? Not knowing who to blame, I became angry with myself and started drinking and getting loaded as a means of escape.

Then early one morning after another long night of partying, I was awakened by a homeowner's sprinklers drenching me from all sides. I had gotten loaded and drunk the night before and had passed out on someone's lawn and had no idea where I was or how I had gotten there. Soaking wet and with a throbbing headache and a mountain of humiliation, I found my way home and got cleaned up.

I sat on the edge of my bed and was forced to admit that I was tired of the life I was living, and yet had no idea how to change it. I wanted to talk to Lilly about the mess my life had become, but was afraid to talk to her.

Worst of all, I realized that the path I was on had little chance of a successful future. Many of my friends were joining the military or going away to college or getting married. I knew that my street life career had worn thin. In sharp contrast, however, I knew that I had a good heart. Most important, I wanted to be much more to my mother than another kid running the street. Amid all my confusion, I wanted to put my head down on my mom's lap where I knew I'd feel safe. It was around that time that I started thinking about God and what was the purpose of my life that Maker wanted me to fulfill.

Although I had become angry with myself and bored with life, I kept going out with Sara and doing my stupid stuff. I never showed her the street side of me, and while she gave the impression that she didn't know about my other lifestyle, the truth was she knew everything. As time passed, I began to wonder why she stayed. Apparently she saw a glimmer of light in me that I couldn't see.

I thought Sara was a strange girl, and her extraordinary intuition made me nervous. She used to say things that would trip me out. At times she almost seemed psychic. Although shy and quiet, she had a way of challenging me. When I'd call her on it, she'd say she was only saying how she felt. She hit some points that angered me, and I'd swell up with my street cockiness and tell her she didn't know what she was talking about. She'd smile and say that was fine.

My dilemma was that Sara was expressing herself through love, which I'd never known or tasted. Her love for me was different from the love my family had for one another. A wise man once said that the most memorable people in our lives will be those who loved us when we weren't very lovable. Looking back, I'll be forever grateful to Sara that she had the stamina and the courage to continue loving me when, indeed, I wasn't very lovable.

Another obstacle that I faced was that I was living a lifestyle based on instilling fear in people. I could scare those around me without even touching them. Outside of my mother, no one had taught me differently until Sara, who had no fear of me and wouldn't allow me to intimidate her. In the deepest part of my being, I began to sense that I was using this power—and the martial arts—in a negative way to selfishly get what I wanted.

The only positive aspect of my life was my karate tournament fighting. In 1973, I fought as a member of Chuck Norris's United Karate Team "The Los Angeles Stars." My teammates were Lenny Ferguson, Manit Chaursan, Manuel Hernandez, my brother Ruben, and my brother-in-law Blinky, who had since married my sister Lilly. Our team fought against other teams that Chuck Norris had formed in five other major cities—the "New York Puppets," "Detroit Dragons," "D.C. Bombers," and the "Texas Gladiators." We took the show on the road, starting in Savana, Georgia, and ending at the LA Sports Arena where the band—"The Shining Star"—was provided by Bruce Lee's brother, Robert.

I continued winning on the noncontact, point tournament circuit; that is, except for when I was disqualified for excessive contact, which wasn't a rare occurrence. At the end of a tournament, I'd walk out with several trophies from wins in single division, katas, team fighting, and Grand Champion. Ironically, after a while, all the trophies looked alike, probably because the promoters were purchasing them from the same manufacturer. Eventually, I became so bored with winning trophies—plus the fact that my mother had no more room in our house to display them—that I gave them to female fans who came to the tournaments to watch me fight.

Once the tournament and all the hoopla ended, everyone would go home, leaving me standing in an empty arena and wondering where I was going and where were all the parties? The reality was there weren't any. The party had ended when the last trophy was handed out. Those who had come to the tournament, both as competitors and spectators, were returning home to prepare for their job or school or something else productive. What I was returning to was regular show where I was the producer, director, and the star. People wanted a show on the dance floor, I'd give them a show. They wanted a show of my street hustle, I'd give them that. They wanted a show of my fighting in Palmer Park with my car club, I'd give them a grand performance!

While in the eyes of many, I gave an Oscar-winning performance, how many times can someone watch the same great movie? After the third screening, not only does the viewer lose interest, but they start noticing the flaws in the picture. My act had grown old, and even I had begun noticing flaws. The way things were going, I had no future, which was a hot button that Sara would occasionally push.

I began seeing my past performance as one big noir movie in which I injured people mentally, physically, and spiritually—and people praised me for it. I wasn't a hero, but people called me a hero. I wasn't special, but people called me special. If people wanted to say I was a five star general for Satan, so be it because maybe that's what I was at the time without knowing it.

I had a lot of anxiety building up. I'd find various outlets like martial arts, football, and dancing that would temporarily burn off steam. This wasn't always the case, however. One afternoon my car club had a football game at Palmer Parker against a motorcycle club called the Midnighters. When a member of the opposing team made a crass remark, I punched the guy squarely in the face, then kicked over a row of motorcycles. Within seconds, a vicious fight broke out that involved more than 100 people. As was usually the case, the cops took their sweet time getting there. Allowing us to beat each other up for 20 minutes meant that we would have less energy to fight the police. Besides, these fights often resulted in thinning out the car club populations.

My walking in the darkness eventually caused me to walk away from Sara and stop answering her phone calls. Within a short time, I felt terribly lonely and distanced myself from practically everyone.

Looking back, it was clear how this had come about. Through my demands and actions, as well as the reactions of others, I stood on a pedestal where I came to recognize the full force of the age-old wisdom "It's lonely at the top." I'd done this to myself. The "looking out for number one" game plan doesn't work. Take advantage of people, use people, be suspicious of everyone, and you are liable to be so successful that you will end up far ahead of everyone else, looking down on them with scorn. And then where will you be? You will be all alone, which is what happened to me.

The loneliness I felt was actually a consciousness feeling of separation from those around me. In time, I felt separated from myself, and in the final stage felt separated from Maker. There is no emotional pain more debilitating than the feeling of consciously being separated from everything and everyone.

It was around this time that a friend of Sara's told her that she had seen me walking down the street holding hands with another girl. Never one to not speak her mind, Sara wrote me a letter that confirmed everything that I suspected had gone astray in my life. According to Sara, I wasn't man enough to be hard-working, honest member of society, the only person I cared about was myself, and that if I didn't make some major changes, my life was going nowhere. This was the first time she had said any of this to me, and I could tell that she meant every word.

At first I laughed, then showed the letter to my younger brother Adam, telling him that for me women were a dime a dozen. I may have fooled him, but I didn't fool myself. Sara was special, and I knew that everything she said was true and that the only reason she said these things was because she cared for me and loved me. None of what she said was out of spite.

Even though I initially laughed at her, I soon became angry. Who was she to tell me that she knew who I really am? Does she think she has something over on everybody? Regardless of my anger, I loved that she wasn't afraid of me and that she would speak her mind and her heart. She was the only one who was upfront with me. When we were out on a date, she'd tell me that she had to be home at a specific time, and as much as I tried to talk her into staying out longer, she wouldn't agree to it. Besides the negative things she said, she told me about the goodness in me and she did this without having an ulterior motive. Most of all, I loved her openness and emotional vulnerability.

The reality that Sara was gone finally sunk in. One night, I sat alone in my garage, drunk and totally wasted, staring at a moonbeam that was shining through a hole in the roof. The hit songs "The Party's Over" and Peggy Lee's "Is That All There Is" could have played over the scene. As I was about to pass out, I watched my tears dripping to the floor and glistening in the moonlight, and I knew at that moment that there was good in me. In the midst of my sadness and confusion, I desperately wanted somebody, anybody to tell me why I'd been born and what my purpose was in life. Following a long silence, darkness came over me.

Sometime later, Lilly found me on the garage floor, unconscious. She was always watching out for me and wondering where I was. "Where's Benito?" I'd often hear her say. She rushed me to the hospital where doctors pumped my stomach. When I finally awoke, I thought I was in heaven because I didn't recognize anything. After I was released from the hospital and returned home, I was so weak and lost that I went to my mother's room and lay on her bed. Thankfully, Lilly promised to not tell my mom that I had been hospitalized.

In the days that followed, I kept thinking about Sara's letter and became so enraged that my jaw hurt from grinding my teeth. Then Sunday afternoon, I was walking alone on Van Nuys Boulevard when some guy said something stupid and swung at me. I went blind on him and beat him badly. The cops were called, and I took off running. By nightfall, I was under arrest for assault, which was upgraded to manslaughter when the district attorney learned that I held a black belt in karate.

Three days later I appeared with a court-appointed public defender and stared down at the floor as I pleaded no contest. When I looked up, I saw Sara and her mother sitting in the courtroom looking at me. In my mind they were making fun of me and thinking *I told you so! You're not man enough!* and throwing it in my face. It was then that I remember Sara telling me that I would never become a better man. The thought enraged me, and I tried to tear loose from my handcuffs, the force being so strong that my wrists bled. When Sara looked at me, I saw tears streaming down her face. I was so distraught that I thought I'd be sick.

I was incarcerated at a county honor farm for just under a year. I was angry the entire time I was incarcerated and stayed to myself. I did what I was told, fought when I needed to survive, ran several miles a day inside the facility, and lifted weights to get buffed.

While incarcerated, I had time to rethink my life. Looking back, I was forced to conclude that all my fast moves, all my manipulating, all my Rico Suave persona, all my wisdom had resulted in my incarceration, totally humiliated, broke, and now without Sara—the only girl who ever truly loved me. Worst of all, I disappointed my family, especially my mother. My father's game plan that all I need do to get ahead in life was to be strong physically, instill fear in people, and not fear anyone or anything was a total and complete lie. I'd come to the realization that I had misused the gift that Maker had given me. I needed to dramatically change my life, and yet I had no idea how I was going to accomplish that.

FOUR

Coming into the Light

▼ ▼ ▼ ▼

The Urquidez Brothers is our name, and why shouldn't we
*   want a little fame?*
People come and people go, but now it's our turn to steal the
*   show.*
As life goes on day by day, we pray the Lord will guide our way.
Let it be known that we have come, but let it be known we come
*   as ONE.*

—Blinky

Since being sentenced in court a year earlier, I hadn't seen or spoken with Sara. When my incarceration ended, I went to Mr. Parker and renewed my training. I never had idols in the martial arts, but Mr. Parker was the closest. I loved his philosophy on fighting and how he went into detail. The fact that he had real-time street fighting experience was important to me.

Mr. Parker arranged for me to teach at his Santa Monica school where I met a young woman student named Linda. Eventually, she became aware of my wanting to change my life and convinced me to join a bible study group that she was attending. She was so eager to help with my salvation that she gifted me with her own personal Bible. Within a short time of joining this study group, my interest in learning about Jesus began to soar.

Apart from the study group, Linda and I met at her home where she would read the Bible to me for hours. One evening, the floodgates opened and I started crying. She moved closer to me, took my hand, and told me that I needed to ask God for forgiveness. Moments later, I felt a rumbling inside, and a warmth came over me. The more I said, "Forgive me, Jesus Christ," the harder I cried, which was truly embarrassing because this was the first time in my life that I had cried. Amazingly, from the moment I asked Jesus for forgiveness, good things began happening in my life, including how I felt inside.

That night when I left Linda's, I drove home with an overwhelming *WOW!* feeling. When I walked into the house, my brothers and sisters looked at me and instantly noticed a change. "Where have you been, Benito?" Lilly asked with a huge smile. "What in the world have you been doing?" Over the next several days, my family noticed a light around me that at times was a bright aura. Lilly was ecstatic and said she'd never seen such beauty in me.

A week later, Mr. Parker sent me to Texas where I taught Kenpo students the fine points of tournament fighting. Everybody wanted me to teach them my spinning back kick. When I later entered full contact kickboxing, I was the first fighter who was able to do damage with it, be accurate with it, and not be afraid to turn my back. In today's MMA fighting, most competitors are afraid to turn their backs. If I were fighting in the cage today, I would still be known for my jump spinning back kick. Not that a lot of fighters aren't throwing spinning back kicks, but they aren't throwing them with the same accuracy and follow through.

A month later, I returned to Los Angeles to fight alongside

The "Urquidez Clan" strong on "Familia"

my brothers in the 1973 Long Beach Internationals, which was now considered among fighters as "the tournament to win." Two media sensations had turned karate into a national pastime, not only for adults, but for children—the unprecedented syndicated television success of "Kung-Fu" starring David Carradine, and Bruce Lee's superstar performance in the blockbuster movie *Enter the Dragon* that had months earlier broken box-office records throughout the world. Carl Douglas' disco song "Kung Fu Fighting" that rose to the top of the American and British charts was the result of the martial arts craze having swept the country.

In addition to entering the team competition, I entered the lightweight black belt sparring competition. Although in the streets of Van Nuys my brothers and I had a notorious reputation,

Top left to right: Arnold, my mother, Ruben, Gene, my cousin Manual, Blinky, Lilly, student. Bottom left to right: myself, Adam, Mando, student. Circa 1974.

on the tournament karate circuit we were highly respected for our sportsmanship and friendly demeanor. When we walked into the Long Beach Sports Arena where champions from throughout the world had gathered, people would comment, "Oh, here's the Urquidez family!"

The high energy level that pervaded the Sports Arena fueled my determination to an all-time level. Arnold looked around and said, "Good, we've got some real competition here." And did we ever! I spent all day Saturday battling my way through the light-weight black belt competition like a Tasmanian devil. At the end of the day, I won my division and semi-finals, which meant that on the following day I'd fight heavyweight Tang Soo Do black belt John Natividad for the coveted Grand Championship.

In August 1973, I was 21 years of age, and John was seven years older and had far more tournament experience. On the night of

My fight with John Natividad is still considered the greatest fight in the 50 year history of the Long Beach Internationals (the referee is Tadashi Yamashita)

the championship fight, 12,000 spectators packed the arena floor to the rafters. Some people were betting that John couldn't match my speed, while others were betting that I couldn't penetrate John's defense because of his excellent technique, footwork, and kicking. The huge building felt as if it would come off its foundation as John Natividad and I put on a clinic that cumulated in an unprecedented 25-point match that went into three overtimes. Amidst a flurry of split-second punches, John delivered a reverse punch to my body as I scored a punch to his head. Ruling that John's punch had arrived a fraction of a second before mine, the judges awarded him the final point and the championship. Ironically, John won the fight by using a technique that I had shown him two weeks earlier. Nearly 50 years later, our fight is considered the greatest noncontact point fighting match ever.

Two major milestones occurred that day. The first was that although I'd always known I was a good fighter, on the day I fought for the 1973 Long Beach Internationals Grand Championship, I knew that I was a great fighter who could battle the best in the country. Second, I'd earned my first honest paycheck, as on that day I received the same $2,500 as the winner, which in 1973 was a king's ransom.

I was on top of the world. I was buffed, driving a new car, decked out in a classy wardrobe, and had money to burn. A year had passed since I'd seen or talked with Sara, and I felt the time had come to show her that everything she had said about me a year earlier was wrong. I'd waited a year for this moment, and actually wanted to spit in her face.

I drove to her house and parked my shiny 240Z where she could see it, then walked to the porch and knocked on her front door with a heavy hand. Sara opened the door, and before I could utter an angry word, sighed "Benny!" and then wrapped her arms around me and started sobbing. She kept telling how much she loved me and that she'd missed me. Her words and the beating of her heart against my chest were like Superman and kryptonite,

Revisiting the bridge at Balboa Park where I proposed to Sara 40 years ago

and in that instant all my anger melted away. It was then that I realized that the reason I'd been so angry with Sara was because I truly loved her and cared about what she thought about me.

A week later, I took Sara to Balboa Park that had a bridge and a lake filled with ducks. I walked to one side of a bridge, stopped her, and told her that we were going to cross the bridge together. When we got to the middle of the bridge, I stopped her again and sang the lyrics from Smokey Robinson's *I'll Try Something New*, "I will build you a castle with a tower so high / Till it reaches the moon / I'll gather melodies from birdies that fly / And compose you a tune." She started crying, and I said, "You're the one for me." We crossed the bridge, and when we reached the other side, I asked her to marry me. Although there had been many girls and young women in and around my life, Sara was my only true girlfriend. That afternoon on the bridge, she became a major part of my new life.

On our wedding day

A year after my championship fight at the Long Beach Internationals, Sara and I were married on August 24, 1974. She was 18 and I was 22. Because we didn't have much money, we had a small, but beautiful, wedding and postponed our honeymoon until we could afford one. As part of my new life with Sara, I promised to stop drinking and getting loaded, which is a promise I've kept to this day.

Our wedding party. Left to right: Sara's brother Robert, Sara's brother Genaro, Lilly, (below Lilly is her son David Urquidez), Blinky, Sara's father Larry Morteo, Sara's mother Connie Morteo, Sara, myself, my mom, Arnold, Sara's brother Charlie, Ruben, Adam "Smiley," and Sara's brother Michael

Our first apartment was a tiny, inexpensive one bedroom that was located by the karate gym where I continued my training. An ugly burnt orange couch that I got for cheap was the focal point of our living room. The couch's end table was a four-foot wide wooden spool that was used to hold thick cable wire. It was adorned with a tablecloth from a secondhand store and a beer bottle that was home to a single flower. We had a used black and white TV, and our bedroom amounted to a mattress

ABOVE: Belgium, present-
ing the two teams

Mr. Parker giving me his
analysis of my opponent

Signing autographs after
the tournament

thrown on the floor. It was all '70s hippie junk, but it was *our* junk.

Sara and I loved being together. On weekends, we'd go to the Starlite Drive-in Theater on Van Nuys Boulevard from money we saved from cashing in empty soda bottles at the grocery store. After we paid to get in, we'd have just enough money to buy popcorn. We'd cuddle in the front seat with our own little picnic and watch the double feature. When we didn't have money, we were happy walking together in the park or spending time at home with friends or at family gatherings. Life was much simpler back then for everyone.

In late 1974, I traveled to Europe and competed in England and Belgium as a member of Ed Parker's 5-member U.S. karate team that was sponsored by Elvis Presley. The other team members, each a proven warrior, were John Natividad, Darnell Garcia, Tom Kelly, and Ron Marchini.

Maker was continuing to bring wonderment to my life. Here I was at the age of 22—and the youngest member of the team— gallivanting throughout Europe like royalty. Elvis loved three things in life above everything else—his mother, his music, and karate. Besides having our own beautifully designed, tailored gis, our team flew first class, stayed in the best hotels, and rode in limousines. Throughout the trip, I was on a tremendous high.

After winning big in England, we traveled to Brussels. The Belgium team was heavily favored by the partisan Brussels crowd, and for good reason—the team was all champions individually, and as a team they were undefeated in Europe. We were told they were rough, tough, experienced, and all business. Fighting alongside some of America's best fighters, I helped beat the formidable fighting teams in England and Belgium. The entire trip was exhilarating. Everywhere I went with the team I felt connected.

After returning home, I continued doing well at noncontact karate tournaments. Fans began treating my fights as if they were rock concerts. Many stood in long lines to buy tickets and drove long distances to get a glimpse of "The Jet" perform his

Top left to right: Steve Muhammad, David Brock, Al Dacascos, Cecil Peoples, John Natividad, Darnell Garcia, and Bob White. Bottom row left to right: Steve Fisher, myself, Mike Stone, and Howard Jackson.

Bottom photo: With legendary Steve Muhammad, cofounder of the Black Karate Federation

Golf Land in Sherman Oaks where in 1974 I earned my first real paycheck. Blinky and I dug that huge hole for the lake.

signature jump spinning back kick. As a result, small and medium sized tournament promoters loved me because, outside the major karate tournament circuit, I was filling the house and almost single-handedly breathing financial life into the fledgling sport of point karate.

There was a problem, however. Aside from fighting in a handful of major karate tournaments that were held annually, there was little money to be made. At best, the majority of tournament organizers awarded trophies, and only occasionally paid a small cash prize. Besides the lack of prize money, the outcome of any fight relied on the judges' ability to accurately award points, which was always up for grabs and often lacked consistency and fairness. As a result, on any given day, any one of a fair list of moderately talented fighters could beat a seasoned champion. Even though I knew I had an edge, there were never any guarantees.

When Sara and I married, I promised her that I could make it in society by getting a regular job that would bring in a steady paycheck. Until this point, the only steady income I ever had was from an assortment of street hustles. Now that I was a responsible married man, I needed to show Sara and her family that I was willing to work to make an honest living.

Down the street from our apartment was a new miniature golf course called Golf Land that was fronted by a huge castle that was visible from the well-traveled San Diego Freeway. Upon reading a job offer ad in the local newspaper that the owner of Golf Land was looking for workers to dig holes and plant trees, I called Blinky, who agreed to apply with me. This was a no-brainer. The work was all physical and would help get us into top shape. Although the pay wasn't much, I was excited to tell Sara that I now had a real job.

Two weeks after I began digging holes at Golf Land, another moment of clarity occurred in my life. When Sara and I married, I made her promise that she wouldn't ask her parents for anything. My pride had kicked in, and I was determined to provide for Sara without anyone's help. While this worked most of the time, it wasn't foolproof. Occasionally, when we would visit Sara's parents, Sara would go to the refrigerator and put a cube of butter or a few slices of bread in her purse. She was hurting for me because I would go to work at Golf Land, and then tell the guys that I was going home for lunch. When I'd arrive home, however, I'd drink water because there was practically nothing to eat, and then return to work.

One morning after I'd left the apartment, Sara cashed in a load of empty bottles at Safeway and bought bread, a can of Campbell's chicken noodle soup, and a ten-cent package of grape Kool-Aid. When I arrived home around noon, she had lunch set out for me—a glass of ice-cold Kool-Aid, a bowl of hot chicken soup, and a bologna sandwich. As I stared at what was to me a lunch fit for a king, Sara smiled, excited and proud that she had done this for her husband.

My initial thought was that she had borrowed money from her mother. "Where did you get this?" I asked in a stern voice.

Sara's smile faded. "I cashed in some bottles."

"There was enough money to buy all this?" I continued, suspecting that she wasn't telling me the full story. As it turned out, I was right. The money she got from cashing in the bottles was enough to buy the can of soup, bread, and package of Kool-Aid—but the package of bologna had been shoplifted by Sara who took two hours to summon the courage to put it in her purse. She'd never stolen anything before in her life. With tears filling her eyes, she told me that she stole the bologna because she didn't want me to go hungry and had cried every time I went back to work without a good lunch.

I was numb. I stood frozen for a long while, and then took her into my arms and promised her that she would never have to do that again. I kept hugging and thanking her, and promising her that I would take care of her. I returned to work feeling like the most blessed man on Earth and determined that my wife would never feel that way again.

This isn't to say that married life, especially my first year, was a breeze; in fact, far from it. The first five years of marriage was

At a press conference prior to a major boxing match. Carlos Palomino is seated on my right, Reverend Jesse Jackson is on my left.

hard, especially the first year because I couldn't get used to answering to Sara. I'd arrive home and she would have dinner for me and ask, "How come you didn't call me?"

I'd get mad and reply, "What are you, my keeper? I have to call you?" Even though I had light in me, I still had some street left.

She'd say, "I'm your wife. Why don't you at least call me?"

I couldn't get it through my head that I had somebody to answer to. I thought only pansies answered to a woman, and I'd say, "You're not my mother. I don't have to answer to you. I'm the man of this house." Often Sara had such insight and would blow me out of the water, and I'd say, "You don't know what you're talking about. Where do you get this stuff from? What do you have people in your head talking?"

She'd reply calmly and matter-of-factly, "Yes."

What truly annoyed me was she would press my buttons an hour before I was walking into the ring. I'd get all worked up and say, "Why is it you always do this right before my fight?!" Then I'd take out my frustration on my opponent. Looking over my fight record, I suppose Sara could argue that I should credit her with a dozen of my knockouts.

While I worked at Golf Land, I was longing for something new that would challenge my fighting ability. Having grown disappointed over the way traditional karate bouts were decided in non-contact karate point fighting, I traded in my gi for a pair of boxing shorts, shoes, and gloves. Having decided to pursue a career as a professional prizefighter, I began training with Super-Featherweight World Boxing Champion Bobby Chacon and Light Welterweight North American Boxing Champion Randy Shields. It wasn't long before many in the professional boxing community felt that I could be another Roberto "Fists of Stone" Duran because of my warrior spirit, my ability to take a punch, my hand speed, and a powerful left hook. During my early sparring sessions with Bobby, he gave me a bloody nose. He was the first person to draw blood from me, and I knew at that moment boxing was what I wanted to do.

To the knockout! As early as 1975 billed as "Karate's New Legend"

I wasn't alone in my zest for more realism in karate tournament fighting. In response to public spectator demand, the idea of full contact soon captured the attention of the nation's karate community. I was helping Bobby Chacon prepare for his title bout when I learned the Professional Kickboxing Association (PKA) had been formed and had started signing fighters to exclusive contracts.

Around that time, I got wind that Tommy Lee, a surfer from Asia, was organizing the first "No weight division / No holds barred World Series of Martial Arts Championships." The event was to take place over a two-day period in Hawaii and was bringing together 58 participants from many different karate styles. The fights would take place in a ring, elbows and knee blows would be allowed, and the winner declared by knockout or decision.

Excited about entering Tommy Lee's full contact tournament, I told Arnold that I'd take a break from my boxing pursuits, go to Hawaii and fight, and then come back and resume boxing. Arnold adamantly said, "No. Either you train in boxing and take the title or you take the title in kickboxing. You can't do both." After much thought, and because I realized that I'd been training in the martial arts since I was eight years old, I decided to see where full contact would take me.

After we were married in August, on November 15, 1974, Sara and I arrived in Hawaii where I fought in Tommy Lee's World Series of Martial Arts World Championship. This was the first time in my martial arts career that I could hit my opponent without being disqualified. Halfway into my first fight, I knew that I was in my element. There's a line between the art of karate and the sport of karate, and a huge difference between noncontact point karate and full contact. Because of my years of real-time street fighting, the instant I hurt my opponent and tasted or smelled blood, my fuse was lit, and I took out my axe and would unleash a relentless, devastating attack.

Besides hitting my opponent in the face, I became known as a body and fender man. Having learned that it's sometimes worse

ABOVE: Sara and I honeymooning in Hawaii after winning the first World Series of Martial Arts Championship

Sara and I used to perform together at Hawaiian Luaus

to get hit in the body than to get hit in the face, I could knock out an opponent with a single body shot. Later I became good at kicking my opponents' legs, which I called his fenders.

The first day of fighting was brutal. Many of the 58 fighters suffered substantial injuries or were knocked out. Ironically, the ring had only one rope, and as a result, opponents were catapulted from the ring and landed hard on the floor or metal chairs. When the second day of fighting began, the majority of fighters had left on the morning airline flights, wanting nothing more to do with full contact karate. After fighting seven different opponents over two consecutive days, and weighing only 145 pounds, I defeated 225 pound Dana Goodson and was crowned the World Champion of all weight divisions of full contact karate.

Having won the Championship purse of $5,000, Sara and I could finally afford our honeymoon, and what better place than in the romantic Hawaiian Islands! When we returned home, I bought her a new car and paid four months' rent in advance. Having finally found my niche in karate and knowing that I could make a good living fighting full contact, I told Sara that she no longer had to work. Because we didn't have children at that time, coupled with Sara's desire to contribute financially to our life together, she took a job as a salesperson.

Five months later on May 10, 1975 in New York, Aaron Banks organized four world championships that were sanctioned by the World Professional Kickboxing Organization (WPKO). I won the lightweight division. The event's organizers had taped the fights and later sold the footage to ABC's "Wide World of Sports."

A week later in Los Angeles at the second edition of the World Series of Martial Arts Championships, I defeated Roland Talton of the Black Karate Federation (BKF) and kung-fu practitioners Bill Henderson, both by KO. Then in June 1975, I won the third and final edition of Tommy Lee's World Series of Martial Arts Championships, defeating Sanun Plypoolsup and Burnis White.

Having continued my study of Christianity, I became convinced that Jesus was a major factor in my winning full contact matches and began thanking Him at the end of each victory, pointing heavenward and stating loudly, "There's power in the blood of Jesus!"

When a television producer of a popular religious program learned of my fight career, my ongoing bible study, and how I was thanking Jesus for my victories, he invited me to appear on his show. I thought it was great, and he sent a camera crew to film my workouts, as well as my studying the Bible and asking God to not allow me to hurt my opponent and how I wanted to perform in God's name and praise His name. The producer also sent a camera crew to one of my fights and filmed me destroying my opponent and then pointing to the sky and saying, "There's power in the blood of Jesus!"

On the day the show aired, Sara and I gathered around our living room TV with family and close friends. The minister who headed up this religious program came on and mentioned kick-boxing champion Benny "The Jet" and ran footage of me jumping rope and shadowboxing. We all thought that was really cool. This was followed by footage of me reading the Bible and asking God to not allow me to hurt my opponent. The next cut was of me beating the daylights out of my opponent, including slow motion footage of blood running down his face. This was shown while cutting back and forth to my reading the Bible and asking God to not allow me to hurt my opponent, then ended with my pointing heavenward and saying, "There's power in the blood of Jesus."

After pausing to allow the show's listeners to absorb the total effect, the minister cited biblical verses that pertained to how people misuse God for their own selfish benefit, coupled with God being abhorred by violence and how Christians are supposed to love their heavenly brothers and sisters and wish them no harm.

The entire show made me look like a hypocrite. I felt used and lied to. We all sat in stunned silence. All of a sudden, tears fell from my eyes, and I walked out and drove to Balboa Park where

I proposed to Sara and sang to her Smokey Robinson's song *I'll Try Something New.*

I sat on that bridge for what felt like an eternity, thinking, *Why, God? Why would someone who claims to be a man of God do that to me?* I was beyond hurt. I was emotionally and spiritually bankrupt.

When I returned home that evening, I asked Sara what she thought about what that minister had done to me, and she said that God had a greater purpose and a better plan for our lives. She also pointed out that due in large part to my Native American heritage, I'm not a religious person, but a spiritual person, and that my journey is really about connecting with my spirituality.

I realize today that what that minister did to me was a blessing because at that time I was so high on being a born again Christian that I'd shied away from the spiritual teachings of my Native American ancestors. A month later, Sara suggested that we try meditation. I agreed, and the more I meditated, the more I started learning and remembering the wealth of knowledge that I'd been born with, but in my early childhood years had forgotten. Essentially, through my first meditations I was going back to my mother's womb and to her teachings, only this time it came back to me in the spiritual realm. Today I recognize that there is only one God, whom I choose to call Maker, but that each of us has to find our own way of connecting to this universal deity.

FIVE

World Kickboxing

B ecause I held the World Series of Martial Arts World Championship title from 1974 to 1976 and then became the PKA lightweight champion, people kept referring to me as the champion of the world. In response, I'd ask, "How can I be champion of the world when I haven't fought outside the United States?"

One day, a kickboxing promoter asked me if I'd be willing to fight Muay Thai, and I immediately replied, "Yeah, I'll fight him!" I thought Muay Thai was the name of a kickboxer. I wasn't ignorant. Although full contact kickboxing originated in Thailand's 2,000 year old discipline of Muay Thai fighting, in the mid-1970s, few people in the States had ever heard of Muay Thai.

Shortly after I said that I would fight Muay Thai, the World Karate Association (WKA International) was created by Howard Hansen (a Shorin-Ryu karate black belt), Mike Stone, and my brother Arnold. At that time, Arnold was considered the utmost authority on full contact karate by professionals throughout the world. As head of the Urquidez Brothers Studio in Panorama

City, his training produced such greats as (besides myself) Lenny "Whirlwind" Ferguson, Ernest "Madman" Russell, and our brother in-law Blinky Rodriguez. The WKA was the first non-profit governing body to use an independently controlled rating list, the first to establish a world championship division for women, and the first to include countries from Asia. The organization became one of the major sanctioning bodies for professional karate. Besides myself, early stars of the WKA included Don "The Dragon" Wilson, Kevin Rosier, and Graciela Casillas.

I was in favor of the WKA because the PKA fighters weren't allowed to kick below the waist. Because the WKA allowed shots to the legs, I developed an arsenal of low kicks and leg sweeps thanks to some strong Asian connections and later fights in Japan. Moreover, because WKA fighters fought internationally, I could fight anywhere in the world.

In early 1977, the WKA and I made martial arts history when we signed to do the first ever Muay Thai fight in the United States that was held on March 12, 1977 at the Olympic Auditorium in Los Angeles. The WKA brought two Muay Thai champions from Thailand to fight nine-round matches as part of the inaugural WKA world title event. Earnest Hart fought in the semi-main event while I waited in my dressing room underneath the arena where I could hear the crowd stomping their feet and yelling "U-S-A! U-S-A! THAI-LAND! THAI-LAND!" I was getting round-by-round updates, pleased to hear that Earnest was winning, when out of nowhere the Thai fighter clocked Earnest—BOOM! A few minutes later, Earnest was carried into our dressing room on a stretcher. I'd never seen anybody so knocked out. I asked him if he was okay, but he couldn't say anything. His eyes had a glazed look, and he was almost cross-eyed. Earnest was a tough fighter, so it was suddenly apparent to me that these Thai fighters must be good if they put Earnest flat on his back, out cold.

Minutes later as Arnold and I made our way through the damp, dingy tunnel and headed toward the ring, I felt like I was

OLYMPIC AUDITORIUM
UNITED STATES CONTACT KARATE
Championships

World kickboxing comes to the United States when I fought the first Muay Thai fighter

walking into steam. It was the kind of heat brought about by a massive outpouring of emotional energy. I entered the ring sporting a shock of long blonde hair and wearing my red pants, which caused the Thai fans to look at me with curiosity. Thai fighters wear shorts. They'd never seen gi pants in the ring, and especially bright red ones with gold braids running down the length of each leg.

As I entered the ring, the crowd again picked up the chant, "THAI-LAND, THAI-LAND, U-S-A, U-S-A!" Moments later, my Thai opponent, Narongnoi Kiatbandit, entered the ring wearing the traditional Thai headwear. I looked at him and thought *that's a nice costume. I should have worn a costume, too.*

Then he started doing Thailand's traditional ceremonial dance (the Ram Muay) that expresses the special relationship of respect and gratitude between a Thai boxer and his trainer and precedes every Muay Thai match. The Ram Muay ritual lasts about five minutes and is performed in rhythm to ringside musical accompaniment.

I watched in awe, then asked Arnold what that was all about. He explained that the guy was praying, and I thought *that's a funny way to pray.* Without thinking, and no doubt due to my years of disco dancing, I started rocking back and forth and prancing around my corner, which the Thai fans took as my making fun of my Thai opponent. About that time, I started smelling a strong aroma coming off the Thai fighter and later learned that it was a special Thai liniment their fighters used to numb their muscles. Narongnoi Kiatbandit had it all over his body.

When the bell rang starting round one, I came face-to-face with the national sport of Thailand for the first time. I watched as their kickboxing champion assume a strange-looking stance. I'd never seen anything like it. He just stood there tapping the mat with his front toe, so I kicked him, but it didn't do anything. Next, I hit him with a ball kick to the body, and he still didn't do anything. This was the first time in my life that I'd hit someone that hard and it didn't budge them.

All of a sudden, he kicked me in the thigh. Ohmygod! I've had Charlie horses before, but I've never had anyone intentionally try to break my leg! Kiatbandit hit me so hard that my eyes bulged and my temples were pulsating. I tried to stay away from his kicks by circling him, but he landed another kick to the same thigh, and then zeroed in on my other thigh. I actually jumped in the air and put my hands down on my thighs in an effort to block them, and then started sticking and moving. The bell rang, and when I got to my corner, I asked my brother what I should do, and he said, "Kick him back!"

Round two began and I started kicking, but Kiatbandit blocked them with his shin. The pain was so excruciating that I couldn't feel my toes, and I started limping. Then I went crazy and charged him with a flurry of punches. He grabbed me by the neck and threw me around the ring like a rag doll, then started kneeing me. The Americans had never seen elbowing and kneeing like this and assumed the Thai fighter was cheating. I thought *okay so you want to street fight. I can do that!* I grabbed him, picked him up and threw him on his head. This upset the Thai fans because this was new to them. Exploding with rage, I launched a barrage of jump spinning back kicks, spinning back fists, change-up kicks—you name it and I landed it while driving Kiatbandit into the ropes. I was hitting him with everything from my bag of tricks, but he kept coming back for more.

Suddenly, I realized that we weren't the only ones fighting. A skirmish had been intentionally started by several Thais who were betting cash by the round, and they owed Arnold a large sum of money. I saw Chuck Norris being attacked by a Thai fan. Chuck nailed the guy, then the entire arena erupted into a full-scale riot. Kiatbandit and I stopped fighting and stood in the center of the ring, totally dumbfounded as we watched a full-scale riot unfold right before our eyes. It felt like I'd suddenly dropped in the Twilight Zone. It was crazy. The audience invaded the ring moments before the final bell. Because the scores were never collected for the final round, the California State Athletic Commission declared a no-contest. As a footnote, I fought Kiatbandit again in Texas and cut his eye so badly that the fight had to be stopped.

When kickboxing began in late 1974, it was called full contact karate. When I fought the Muay Thai champion at the Olympic Auditorium, because few people had any idea what I was doing, I was often asked, "So you kick and box?"

I'd reply, "Yes, exactly. Kicking and boxing." That was how the word kickboxing was born in the United States.

I already had a name in noncontact, point fighting, and after a year of fighting full contact, I began openly stating to the world kickboxing community, often when interviewed on network television, that I would fight any fighter in *their* country, under *their* rules, and that the fight would be judged by *their* judges. No other fighter anywhere was making this statement that essentially amounted to an open challenge.

Sara enjoying her baby shower. Love my preppy college sweater!

Years earlier, kickboxing had become popular in Japan and in 1970 was telecast in Japan three times weekly on three different television channels. The fight cards regularly included bouts between Japanese kickboxers and Muay Thai boxers. Intrigued by my open challenge, Japan's reigning kickboxing champion, Katsuyuki Suzuki, agreed to fight me.

In July 1977, I arrived with Blinky in Tokyo, Japan, along with four other American kickboxers who had signed on to fight the semi-main events. My immediate reaction to this mystical land of the samurai was that I felt like I was home, and yet I wasn't. In a strange way, I felt as if I'd been there before, many centuries ago. The feeling was one of being grounded.

An hour later, along with the four other American fighters, I was put up in Japan's most luxurious hotel. Blinky and I shared the same room. Suddenly, he remembered the premonition from God that I had ten years earlier that foretold that Blinky and I would one day travel the world together. We were so overwhelmed by Blinky's recollection that we decided to pray. The windows were open, and as we prayed, the wind outside suddenly began to blow so hard that the tall, thin trees outside began to bend so severely that we feared they would snap. An instant later, the wind became powerful gusts that blew into our room and sent the curtains sailing up to the ceiling. The profound experience was incredibly surreal and empowering.

After a week of pre-fight training, on August 2, 1977, our five-member team was taken to Japan's renowned Nippon Budokan Hall (the name literally means Japan Martial Arts Hall). Although the Budokan had been used as a venue for big musical events, its primary purpose had been for Japanese martial arts. When in 1966 the Beatles became the first rock group to perform at the Budokan, their appearance was met with strong opposition from those who felt the performance of a western pop group would defile the venerable martial arts arena.

Earlier at the weigh-in, I was told that Suzuki had little, if any, respect for my fighting ability and felt that my prior knockouts

Japan when I fought Kunimatsu Okao. The two teams being introduced

had been a matter of luck. Besides Suzuki's disdain for my ability, it was well known that the Japanese thought little of American kickboxers. The Japanese come from a long lineage of strict Shotokan karate dating back to Old Japan and its highly skilled samurai swordsmen. Because of Japan's deep history, I felt tremendously honored to be the first American to defend a world title at the Budokan, which was Japan's arena of warriors. I knew at that moment that if I didn't knock Suzuki out, I would lose the match.

On the night of the five-card event, 15,000 spectators were in attendance. One by one, the first four of our American five-member team were defeated. I was the last fight and would be defending my WKA Super Lightweight Championship title. When I appeared in the ring wearing long pants, the Japanese officials argued that I had to wear shorts. I told them that I was a traditional martial artist and that I wear pants, not shorts. Finally, the judges ruled that I could wear pants because, so I was later told, they thought that I was going to get knocked out, anyway.

When I met Suzuki in the middle of the ring before the start of the fight, I could tell by the look in his eyes that to him this fight was more a matter of honor than sport.

When the bell rang starting round one, I knew that Suzuki planned on taking my legs from me. But because of my prior experience fighting the Muay Thai fighter at the Olympic Auditorium, I had become skilled in defending and countering against leg attacks. After three rounds of fighting, it was clear that Suzuki was no match for my superior boxing skills that I had honed through my training with Bobby Chacon. My spinning back kicks and crushing body punches wore Suzuki down. In round four, I took my axe and started chopping, dropping him several times through round five. In round six, I knocked him down again, and he staggered to get up, clutching onto the ropes. If this fight had taken place in the United States, the referee would have stopped it, but not in Japan. Left with no alternative, I delivered a left hook to Suzuki's face that knocked him unconscious. It took several minutes to revive him. Stunned silence came over the 15,000 Japanese spectators as they watched me execute my signature backflip. My victory was the first championship belt ever recognized in Japan.

When I beat Suzuki, Japan's former undefeated champion, Kunimatsu Okao, came out of retirement and formally challenged me that same night. There was no question that he was determined to restore honor to his country's stable of highly revered kickboxers. He was a famous Japanese champion with 60 fights under his belt, and 50 of those by knockout.

Three months later on November 14, 1977, I returned to the Budokan to fight Kunimatsu Okao, who was such a big name in Japan that he didn't even come to the weigh-in. On the morning of the fight, I stood on the scale, looked around and asked, "Where's my opponent? How come he's not here?" The officials

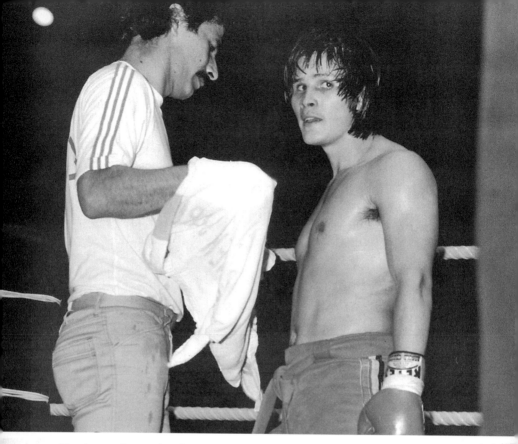

You just woke up the sleeping giant!

casually told me not to worry and that Okao would be at the fight.

That night when I saw Okao enter the ring, I said to Arnold, "This guy's not 142," referring to his weight, "This guy's gotta be easy 165. Look at his legs. This guy is huge." My brother told me to watch out for Okao's legs, that they were very powerful. I said, "Okay, brother, I got it."

The bell rang, and we both came to the center of the ring and started moving around. Thirty seconds into the round, Okao made a slight movement with his lead leg, almost like a twitch, and when I looked down, he hit me with a powerful overhand right that nearly tore my head off and dropped me. He looked down at me sprawled on the canvas, and I could see he had a smirk on his face. I immediately jumped up, shook it off, and smiled at him as I thought *you just woke up the sleeping giant!*

I was sure at that moment that he thought I was finished because he'd easily knocked me down within the opening minute of round one. On the other hand, he had to be concerned that he'd clobbered me with his best shot and it clearly had little effect on me.

The next two rounds were nonstop back and forth, as we traded our best kicks and punches. Okao was a formidable opponent and much stronger and faster than Suzuki. At one point, I blocked one of his kicks that he delivered so hard that the impact on my blocking arm lifted me a foot off the ground.

At the end of round three, my brother asked how I was doing, and I told him, "I feel good, brother."

He knew me well and could see the intense, determined look in my eyes. "I don't have to tell you how to fight this guy. Just do what you love to do."

Halfway into round four, I knew that I had hurt Okao and

Landing a kick during the Okao fight

Moments after I knock out Okao, the ref pulls me back

Sara and Ruben join me in the center ring

went into the zone. After a series of crushing body shots, I heard him wheeze several times that indicated his respiratory system was in spasm. I went after him like a crazy man, hammering him with kicks and punches and finally pinning him on the ropes. An instant later, as the crowd stood and began yelling, I knocked him out with a vicious left hook. He was unconscious before he hit the canvas.

While his corner men rushed to his side with the physician, I did my victory backflip as Blinky, my mother, and Sara stepped into the ring to celebrate with me. I had just beat Japan's second champion and became a sports hero and celebrity to the Japanese. Convinced that I couldn't have defeated both their champions without having Japanese blood in my veins, I became known throughout Japan as the great "Yukiide-san," whose meaning denotes that I'm half Japanese.

On February 27, 1978 Sara gave birth to our beautiful daughter Monique. She was a planned pregnancy, and Sara and I, as well as our families, were overjoyed and felt blessed to have her in our lives.

Two months after Monique was born, I returned to Japan to fight another of their champions, this time Japan's number one contender, Shinobu Onuki. The Japanese were determined to bring the title to Japan. Prior to the fight, Chuck Norris, whose film career

1981 with "Daddy's Little Girl" Monique

was taking off, was introduced to the crowd, as well as mention of his recently released movie *Breaker, Breaker*. Because Monique was only two months old, Sara stayed home, although Lilly and my mom traveled to Japan to be at the fight. Unfortunately, the fight had to be stopped when Inoki injured his shoulder from a throw. What I'll always remember about this fight is that following Inoki's injury, he appeared at my dressing room with his entourage and gifted me with a bouquet of flowers. Throughout my kickboxing career, the Japanese stood out for their humility and sportsmanship. They are truly honorable people.

ABOVE: With Bill "Superfoot" Bill Wallace and my top student Petie "Sugar-foot" Cunningham; BELOW: With Richard Norton

A page from the Japan's comic book that featured me as the hero

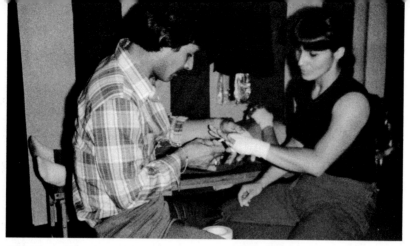

One of my favorite pictures of Lilly watching Arnold tape her hands. I fought right after her fight.

In January 1980, Onuki and I met for a rematch at the Tropicana Hotel in Las Vegas. Although he was a strong warrior and hit me with several good shots, I won the fight by knockout in the seventh round. With the arrival of 1980, I had become a hero in Japan, especially to the children, as evidenced by a series of popular cartoons and comic books that feature me.

Because my fights were always sold out, promoters were confident that they couldn't lose money on a Benny "The Jet" fight. As an footnote, I earned more money in one fight in Japan than any of the American kickboxers made for the entire year. Because of my box-office success, I was able to open doors to other countries that were then open to other American kickboxers.

My life as a world champion kickboxer wasn't without its problems, especially given the high degree of public visibility and earnings. As I approached the 1980s, my head started getting so big that I felt as if I were back in the street. Every country I traveled to, I was offered women, booze, and dope. Promoters put me up in lavish hotel suites and would whisk me away from the hotel whenever I brought my wife and mother with me. These businessmen would say we needed to leave to discuss business, and then they'd pull up to a geisha house or similar den of ill repute. They somehow chose not to hear me when I'd tell them that I didn't smoke, drink or do drugs, and that I was happily married.

When it came to the well-meaning, general public, I couldn't

Lilly and Blinky, the only husband and wife kickboxing team

walk along the streets or go into a restaurant without being sur-rounded by fans pressing me to sign autographs. Chefs would want me to sign plates, and the owners would give me their card and tell me that I was carte blanche and that my money was no good in their establishment. The problem was I truly wanted to pay for things. Getting something without working for it wasn't part of my new life with Sara.

I got to the point where I said, "Sara, be with me and save me" because I felt the darkness coming back. I'd been through the dark side and now was living in the light. But now those who live in the dark were trying to pull me back into the darkness by offering me the trappings of fame and fortune. What I learned was that when a person decides to leave the darkness and walk into the light, dark forces will try to destroy them by attacking them physically, emotionally, and spiritually. Through my dealings with the super wealthy who appear to live in the light, I learned that many of these people are as evil as those who openly live on the dark side. I realized I didn't want to be rich and famous if it was going to mean a return to the darkness with all its loose women, dope, booze and a lifestyle of mistrust and intimidation. I walked out of the darkness and was now leading a spiritual life in the light. Had it not been for Sara and her Native American medicine, Satan might have suc-ceeded during this time in pulling me back into the darkness.

I'd known for a long time that Sara grounded me, which is why I asked her to stay close to me. Wherever we traveled, she took me to churches and other spiritual places. I absolutely loved going with her. While this was helpful, however, I felt that I needed more. My martial arts had taken me a long way, yet after spending time at these spiritual sanctuaries, I felt driven to short-en the gap between my having become a martial arts celebrity and my need to be a part of the everyday martial arts community. I needed to establish balance in my art that would then transfer to my life. The solution was that I needed to spend less time *doing* the art and get back to *teaching* the art. I fought because I could; I teach because teaching is my passion.

SIX

The Jet Center

O ne of several nicknames that Blinky has given me over the years is "The Doodling King from New Orleans." In 1980, I started giving thought to building a kickboxing center that would be far more than the average martial arts dojo. For several days, I spent my spare time sketching what I envisioned as a kickboxing mini-camp and showed these doodles to Blinky. He took one look at them and said, "Count me in."

At that time, I was teaching a student named Jan Serchuck, who was a building contractor. When Blinky and I showed Jan my sketches, he also wanted in. Together the three of us found an old, abandoned building that years earlier had been a bowling alley but now was home for dozens of derelicts and drug dealers. Having agreed on the terms of purchase, we closed a two-day escrow and were handed the keys.

I've always been a construction worker at heart and have never owned a martial arts gym or home that hasn't undergone a complete remodel. After assembling a demolition slash construction crew, we went to work tearing apart the building.

Over the course of several months, carpenters, plumbers, electricians, plus a wide array of professional craftsmen, worked around the clock. Investing a small fortune into the venture, we turned that ramshackle bowling alley into a beautiful single purpose building that could rival the best health clubs in Los Angeles.

During the finishing stages of the renovation, I was in China while Blinky oversaw the work. People were forever stopping by to see how things were going, and with few exceptions kept asking the same two questions. In response, I had grey T-shirts made for the construction workers, family, and staff that displayed these two questions on front: (1) "When's Benny Coming Back?" and (2) "When you gonna open?" and when the wearer of the T-shirt turned around, one word—"SOON!"—answered both questions. Needless to say, those shirts got a great laugh and today are considered collector's items.

When I returned from China, Blinky brokered a $525,000 bank loan for operating capital, and what became known as "The Jet Center" finally, amid robust fanfare, had its grand opening. Pleased that the old bowling alley that was once an eyesore and

With Ruben, Blinky, and Jan Sercheck, who is now married to my niece, Arnold's daughter.

A view from my upstairs office of the Jet Center's 3,000 sq. ft. main floor

the armpit of Van Nuys had been turned into an upstanding business enterprise, grateful members of the City Council showered us with praise and official community awards.

The Jet Center had the feel of a high-class health spa. Two elevated, full-sized boxing rings were the focal point of the Center's 3,000 square foot main hardwood floor and 25-foot ceiling. Throughout the Center, majestic trophies and championship belts were prominently displayed. One entire wall of the Center was called the "Wall of Fame" and was reserved for photos of Hollywood actors, championship fighters, politicians, royalty, and other celebrities from many different countries, cultures, and lifestyles. The overall look of this particular area of the Center resembled a kickboxing museum. Also at the front entrance was Blinky's Café that served only health food, as well as a sports store and pro shop that sold our own training equipment and the Jet Center's personal clothing line.

The second floor of the Center housed the offices that included my personal office, a sports medicine facility, and a control booth that controlled member traffic. One door led into the Jet's

Taken at the Jet Center with Blinky, myself, and many of our gym members and stable of fighters

Gym, while another led to the "Doorway of Knowledge," and so forth. A state-of-the-art weight room and dormitories for overnight and extended-stay guests were also located on the top floor. Men and women had their own dressing facilities, each area being equipped with saunas, Jacuzzis, shower stalls, lockers, Japanese baths, and beautiful mosaic-tiled vanities with hair blowers.

We promoted our own kickboxing matches at the Jet Center

With Eric Lee at the Jet Center wearing my customized Jet Wear line of clothing

that were open to the public. In addition, we trained and managed our own stable of world-class fighters. When the Center wasn't promoting fights, Blinky was cutting deals with television and movie producers who leased the Jet Center for use as an interior set. In view of the myriad of ongoing activities at the Jet Center, working at the Center was akin to taking a college course in Business 101.

A year after our grand opening, hundreds of the best martial artists from dozens of systems and styles were drawn to the Jet Center because I was the one who had for years been promoting kickboxing throughout the world and was teaching my own kickboxing system. In the 1980s, I designed a style of kickboxing that everybody could learn and a curriculum through which everyone could see their personal growth. The difference from earlier methods of kickboxing was that I was teaching both the external and internal aspects of the sport, thus giving it balance. The key was learning the external physical combat, the

Posing with my six championship belts

internal emotional combat, *and* the balance of how to use it to enrich one's life.

Prior to the Jet Center opening, throughout my fighting career I filmed my fights and studied my opponents' techniques and made them more effective. In addition, over time I modified many of my own techniques, especially my round kicks.

With each fight, I used myself as a human guinea pig. For example, when I fought Suzuki, he threw elbows at me that I didn't see coming. I'd never seen that technique before. After the fight, I studied the fight footage and saw how he was using his rotor cup and taught myself how to do that, as well as developing a way to block the technique. When I fought Okao, although I'd mastered Suzuki's technique of delivering elbows and had also perfected my side kicks, I still didn't understand how Okao was doing his inside outside kicks and switching knees on me. Moreover, I didn't know how to block that particular maneuver or get away from it. After studying the fight footage, I saw what Okao was doing when he clinched me and developed a way to successfully counter that particular move.

After years of writing and collecting notes, I assembled all my observations, and in 1982 wrote *Practical Kickboxing: Strategy in Training & Technique* that was published by Pro Actions Publications. Besides outlining my own unique style of kickboxing, the book provided an excellent understanding of the basic kickboxing techniques, as well as advanced combinations, fighting techniques, strikes, focus pads, the medicine and speed balls, Thai pads, the power shield, and punching bags. Since 1982, I have written five books, and to this day *Practical Kickboxing: Strategy in Training & Techniques"* is considered the kickboxing bible in every country. Not surprisingly, keeping the book in stock at the Jet Center was a monumental task.

Because I was busy teaching, writing, and working in the film industry, Sara took over running the daily operation of the Jet Center, although Blinky was the Center's director. After six

On my Panhead Harley with Sara outside the Jet Center

My book on kickboxing that to this day is considered the kickboxing bible throughout the world

months, Sara and I realized that there was so much money going through the Center—tangible money—that we didn't know what to do with it all. We were young and in our late-20s, and neither one of us had any experience running a business enterprise the size and complexity of the Jet Center. Thankfully, because of my high visibility as a worldwide prizefighter, I was a magnet to entrepreneurs and investors who wanted to go into business with me in one form or another and made themselves, and their expertise, available to me whenever I found myself up against a business dilemma.

After the first year, and thanks in large part to television, radio, and magazine coverage, the Jet Center became known around the world as the mecca for the fighting arts. Because of the enormous media coverage, people were coming from all walks of life, including physicians, housewives, politicians, attorneys, blue collar workers, students, military personnel, law enforcement, film and television celebrities, and civil service workers. Once a person

With 8-time heavyweight World Champion kickboxer Australian Stan "The Man" Longinidis and Professor Toru Tanaka

entered the Center, however, the Jet floor had no caste system. Everyone arrived at the Jet Center knowing that it was time to sweat and work and a time to grunt, so there was a balance. Key throughout the Center were honor and respect. Profanity was not allowed.

Another aspect that made the Jet Center unique was that when it came to dojos, the Center was in a league of its own. Back in the late 1950s during the inception of karate in America, and for the next two decades, most karate dojos were located in small commercial rental spaces, often in strip malls. Usually, these karate schools amounted to a small mat area with mirrors, public viewing area, small office with a phone and a half-dozen plaques on the wall, a lackluster dressing area, and a unisex restroom. The more upscale dojos had showers. Because these schools were open only in the afternoons when schools let out, in the evenings Mondays through Thursdays, and for a few hours on Saturdays for children's classes, the majority of school owners couldn't afford to pay more than five-hundred dollars per month in rent. Looking at the full picture, these dojos were unattractive and in some cases depressing.

The Jet Center, on the other hand, was an upscale dojo that catered to some of the wealthiest clientele in the greater Los Angeles area. Compared to the average Motel-6 dojo of the day, coming to train at the Jet Center was like checking into a suite at a Ritz-Carleton Hotel. When the Center opened in the 1981, LA's 1960s hippie and 1970s disco generations had been replaced by the Yuppie generation of 76-million over-indulged egocentric Boomers who poured onto Wall Street beginning their upwardly mobile perfectionist careers. As a result, the crash-pad dojo of the bygone eras had been replaced by the classy Jet Center with all its bells and whistles. By the mid-1980s, the Jet Center had become so popular that we almost had to conduct hourly tours.

Being young and impressionable, there were times when I, myself, got caught up in all the hoopla of the new Yuppie generation mindset, particularly when I was being paid large sums

Muhammad Ali showing me the "Sweet Spot"

ABOVE: Demonstrating my jump spinning back kick before a crowd at the Jet Center, BELOW: With Kenpo Master Bob White on our trip to Romania

of money for the use of my name and likeness. Working as my manager, Blinky would come to me and ask how much I wanted to endorse a particular commercial product, how much I wanted to teach or give a lecture, or how much I wanted to appear in a motion picture or television commercial. When I first opened the Jet Center, except as a kickboxer, I had no idea as to the amount of money people were willing to pay me. As I grew older and wiser, however, I recognized that my life was worth a whole lot more than what I once thought it was.

Up to that time, the 1980s was my greatest period of growth and when I truly came into myself. I was solid and into the zone of my career. Everything was working wonderfully, and I was enjoying earning a good living and traveling the world. I had come a long way from living on Bunker Hill in that tiny two-bedroom apartment with my parents and eight brothers and sisters. And I had certainly made good on my promise to Sara that I would earn an honest paycheck and become an upstanding member of society.

Sara and I were enjoying life. Because of my success, we went where we wanted to when we wanted to. Although she had the best of everything and our daughter attended the finest schools and had anything she wanted, I realized that because of my extensive traveling, I

Our beautiful daughter Monique, age 10

had truly missed spending quality time with my family.

At the time when I was so busy with work, Sara would say, "You don't need to go there" and "We don't need any more money, it's family time" and "I don't care about these actors and directors who call. This is our time. Tell them you'll call them later." Looking back, I'm grateful to my wife that she stuck to her guns and enforced the fact that when it's family time, it's family time. Now that I'm a doting grandfather, I'm truly aware of my grandson's need to spend quality time with Grandpa.

On April 12, 1992, I was overcome with tremendous sadness when my mother passed away at the age of 82 after a brief illness. For many years, she lived with Lilly and Blinky at their home in Sylmar. Many in our family were at her side on the day she passed. I sat on the side of her bed while she spoke to us about what had been the driving force throughout her life—the importance of familia, which reiterated what Sara had been talking about for months. In a soft voice and a peaceful look in her eyes, my mom shared with us her last wish that we wouldn't fight among ourselves and that we would continue to love and help one another. Along with the other family members, I promised my mother that I would do as she asked. Then she turned to the television to watch her favorite movie *The King and I.* A while later, Sara looked at me and said in a loud whisper, "Your mom!" I looked down and saw that my mom had died in my arms. Sara said that she had seen my mother's last breath. That moment was so precious to me. All the fame and fortune in the world could never replace it.

Days later, I gathered with my family at the San Fernando Mission Cemetery where we all said our final farewells to our mother. As I stood at my mom's grave, I knew that she was proud of me and my accomplishments. Since I was a child, she had told me that I had a gift and that I was the chosen one who would plant our flag. It was true that I was the one that my mom and siblings put their money in the hat and sent off into the world to use my warrior skills. Over time, I opened many doors for

My true hero in her late 70s

members of my family that afforded them the opportunity to earn considerable money. As I watched my mother's casket being lowered into her final resting place, I hoped that she realized that everything I did was out of love and respect for her and in return for the unconditional love, protection, and support that she had given to me throughout my life.

SEVEN

Hollywood

Since I was a child, my mother and Lilly told me that I was a natural actor. A year after I started my karate training with Bill Ryusaki, I began participating in karate demonstrations that were usually geared at drumming up new students. After a dozen demonstrations, I realized that the key to giving a great karate demonstration was winning over the audience by capturing their emotions. With practice, I became good at knowing when and how to keep an audience quiet, how to gradually fuel their emotions, and how to deliver an explosive finale that would release their pent up emotional energy.

When I began my fighting career in noncontact point karate, winning over the spectator crowd was important because their collective energy influenced both the judges and my opponent. Having a crowd rocket to its feet and unleash a raucous cheer whenever I scored a point weakened my opponent's confidence. When I became involved in Hollywood filmmaking, my years of giving karate demonstrations and years of competing in tournaments and kickboxing title fights was akin to years of classes in acting and film directing. The methods I used to capture the live energy of thousands of karate spectators were the same methods I used when I stood before a movie camera. To me, inside that camera was a live audience that was no different from the live audience at Japan's Budokan.

To millions of filmgoers, Bruce Lee is the greatest icon of martial arts cinema and a key figure of modern popular media. Had it not been for Bruce Lee and his movies of the early 1970s, it's arguable whether or not the martial arts film genre would have ever penetrated and influenced mainstream North American and European cinema and audiences the way it has over the past four decades

On August 19, 1973—a month after Bruce Lee's tragic passing—*Enter the Dragon* opened at the world-renowned Grauman's Chinese Theater in Hollywood and broke all existing box-office records in its first week, and then proceeded to sweep across the nation in a whirlwind of rave reviews. To this day, *Enter the Dragon* stands as the highest grossing martial arts movie of all time, having

With Blinky and Ruben on the set of *Force: Five*

turned an $850,000 budget into more than a billion dollars in viewer revenue.

Within a nanosecond after the worldwide release of *Enter the Dragon,* practically every Hong Kong and Hollywood producer tried to duplicate its astronomical box-office success. Throughout the world, actors of all shapes and sizes, and all nationalities, were attempting to become the new Bruce Lee. Even those who had never taken a karate lesson were banging on the doors of Hollywood and Hong Kong producers begging for an audition.

In the late 1970s, I was approached by the director Robert Clouse and producer Fred Weintraub, who were the director/ producer team behind *Enter the Dragon.* They were producing a film called *Force: Five* whose story and lead casting basically mirrored the formula of *Enter the Dragon.* They offered me a role in the film, and after reading the script, I agreed to do the picture along with the other four members of the 5-member Force team—Joe Lewis, Richard Norton, Bong Soo Han, and Sonny Barnes, who were also accomplished martial artists.

When *Force: Five* began principal photography, I was eager to perform whatever action fight sequences that director Bob Clouse wanted. One day early in the shoot, he asked if I could fall down a flight of stairs, and I said, "Absolutely!" I fell down the stairs, and then he asked me if I could do it again for another camera angle, and I again said, "Absolutely!" After falling down that flight of concrete stairs a half-dozen times, I was starting to get sore. That was when I found out that stuntmen, and actors who perform their own stunts, wear pads under their clothing.

The film's stunt coordinator looked at me and said with bewilderment, "You're not wearing pads?"

"No. Am I supposed to be wearing pads? What are pads, anyway?"

These people assumed I had pads on and no doubt were thinking *who would be brave enough to fall down a flight of concrete steps a half dozen times without pads?* The Jet, that's who! This real-time rough-and-tumble wasn't new to me, given my years of street fighting experience, as well as my being a proficient gymnast and martial artist. That's why they call me "The Jet." I love speed. I love fast cars and fast motorcycles. I love the thrill of danger, and I especially love new challenges.

As a stuntman and stunt coordinator, I must be willing and able to do many things that most people would be afraid to do. But to me, there's a blessing in this. Throughout my life, even when I was a child, whenever someone asked, "Who wants to go first?" not only did I raise my hand, but I'd already be walking forward because I wanted the blessing of knowing what the emotional rush would be like and what caused it. By becoming willing to do something that my mind perceives as threatening to my survival, only then can I get to the root of how the physical/mental/spiritual mechanism works that causes me to be fearful.

Because of my belief, directors and stunt coordinators knew there wasn't anything that I was unwilling to try. While some people felt that my overconfidence might result in my being seriously injured or even killed, with rare exception, every take was right on the money, which is why directors and stunt coordinators began calling me "The one take kid."

I fell in love with Hollywood from the first moment I set foot on a sound stage. I loved its high energy level, the creative process that strove for perfection, and the grand sense of humor of so many of those I worked with. Having come from the projects, Hollywood's glamorous lifestyle and lucrative pay scale were highly appealing. After a while, I became accustomed to riding in limousines, eating at the finest restaurants, and staying in the best hotels when on location. While it was true that I was treated well by prizefight promoters, as a member of the Screen Actors' Guild, my union's Minimum Basic Agreement dictated that I be treated like royalty.

A week before *Force: Five* was to be released worldwide, I arrived in Hong Kong on a press junket to promote the film. While I was appearing on a late night talk show, a guy stood up in the studio audience and loudly called me nothing but an actor and a

Laughing it up with martial arts icon Gene LeBell

sham fighter! My initial reaction was that I thought it was a prank that the producer had conjured up, until I learned that the guy shouting in the audience was Hong Kong's kickboxing champion. Puffing out his chest, in his next tirade he openly challenged me to fight him the following day.

Had this occurred in the United States where talk shows are taped, the director would have called for a cut, the crew would have been put on hold while the guy was removed from the studio, and that would have been the end of it. The television show in Hong Kong, however, was broadcast live, which meant that this man's open challenge had been heard by tens of thousands of viewers. Thinking the easiest way out of this public relations nightmare was to call the guy's bluff, I told him I'd fight him for $20,000 US dollars and a mink coat for my wife.

The ploy didn't work. The next morning, this guy's manager showed up at my hotel with a platinum mink stole and a manila envelope containing $20,000 in 100 dollar bills. Along with a couple hundred paying spectators, his Hong Kong kickboxing champion was waiting for me in a nearby warehouse, ready to fight. The manager had very cleverly promoted a fight between his fighter and the world champion Benny "The Jet." Knowing that if I didn't show up, word would spread throughout Hong Kong that I was a no-show, I deposited the man's money and fur coat at the hotel's main desk for safe keeping, and climbed into an awaiting taxi.

A half hour later when I entered the warehouse, I felt as if I'd walked into a fight scene depicted in the movie *Blood Sport* starring Jean-Claude Van Damme. The place was dark, damp, and reeked of stale fish. Several hundred Chinese were pressed around a makeshift ring with no ropes. I figured I would make short work of this guy's fighter by injuring him bad enough that he'd quit or his manager would stop the fight and drive me back to my hotel.

I removed my coat and walked to my corner while staring across the ring at my opponent. Moments later, a horn sounded and this square-jawed Chinese kickboxing champion approached me with his arms thrust upwards. Above the spirited banter of hundreds of onlookers, most of them wielding handfuls of cash, my opponent screamed, "To the death!"

Did I hear him correctly? Suddenly, I realized from the fierce look in his eyes that he had every intention of killing me. As we met in the center of the ring, foam collected on my lips and sweat slipped off my chin as I realized I was in a fight for my life. The street in me kicked in, and I instantly went into the zone. I sent a kick grazing across his cheekbone, followed by a kick that smashed into his ribs.

By the end of the first round, my opponent had absorbed considerable punishment, and by the end of round three he looked like Elephant Man. In round four, my repeated rib shots laid the guy on his back, spasmodically sucking air. The crowd clamored around the ring, shouting and whistling. They wanted a kill, and I wouldn't give it to them. With tempers starting to flare, the promoter pulled me into an adjoining room where I waited

Working on the film *Con Air*

for an hour before the near-riot subsided and the crowd left the warehouse.

Over the past 33 years, I've worked on over 50 motion pictures, 24 as an actor and 28 as a stuntman and fight coordinator. In looking at this large body of work, I'm best known for the two films that I did with Hong Kong's cheeky, lovable, and best known film star, Jackie Chan, who has been described as a three-way hybrid of Bruce Lee, Buster Keaton, and Charles Chaplin. Jackie's martial arts skills, phenomenal death-defying stunts, as well as his physical comedy and light humor are what set him apart from all the Bruce Lee imitators that followed the death of the legend.

I appeared in two movies with Jackie Chan. The first was in 1984 called *Wheels on Meals,* the second was in 1988 called *Dragons Forever.* Of the two, I'm best known for my role as Mondale's henchman in *Wheels on Meals.* In the climatic fight scenes in both movies, I'm depicted as a relentlessly tough opponent who is in-

Jackie Chan and I during a light moment on the set of *Wheels on Meals*

evitably defeated. My final fight with Jackie in *Wheels on Meals* is to this day considered to be among the finest fights of his career and the fight sequences that everyone is trying to match.

Jackie Chan and I were extremely physical in the two films we did together because with Hong Kong style films, audiences want to *feel* the action, as opposed to Western style martial arts films in which theatergoers want to *see* the action. When Jackie hit me in the face, his blows were nearly full force. Because I didn't want to risk having the camera see my mouthpiece, I'd take it out and stuff my mouth with tissue paper and let Jackie wail away. These fights were by no means a one-sided. When it became my turn to unleash kicks and punches on Jackie, he willingly took many solid hits.

Because we were both striving to get as close to realism as we could, after a while our encounters had escalated to the level that many of the cast and crew thought we had it out for each other. Then one day during a break, we were sitting together and Jackie said with a straight face, "So, when do you want to fight me for real?"

I looked at him with surprise and said, "You want to fight me?"

"Yes," Jackie repeated, again with a straight face.

"I do this for a living, you know," I replied, figuring that he would confess that he was joking, but that didn't happen.

We continued shooting for two more weeks, during which time rumor of Jackie challenging me to a fight and my accepting his challenge had circulated among the cast and crew. When we arrived at the end of the film, we were again sitting together, and he again brought up fighting me. All around us there was suddenly dead silence. I looked at him and said, "You can't be serious. I'm telling you, I fight for a living." Jackie looked at me sternly, and then I detected the hint of a smile turning the corners of his mouth. I said, "We're not really fighting, are we." Jackie broke out laughing and admitted he'd been joking all along. To this day, Jackie and I are still laughing about that. We have great respect for each other. At the end of *Wheels on Meals,* we gave each other a big hug.

Over the years, many people have asked me why *Wheels on Meals* wasn't called *Meals on Wheels,* which seemed far more fitting. The reason is due to Chinese superstition. Prior to producing *Wheels on Meals,* Golden Harvest had produced two films beginning with "M"—*Megaforce* (1982) and a film titled *Menage a Trois,* both of which were major flops. Because of this, the company's executives changed the title hoping this film would avoid the same problems, which it did.

To me, the martial arts isn't solely about punching and kicking. It's a way of life in which I see myself as a warrior. Physically striking an opponent is the exterior aspect of the art. When I perform a fight scene in a movie, I want to touch the viewer's mind and soul, which is what I call inside out. The best way I know to do this is to make the actor look so real that the audience perceives or *feels* the actor *is* real.

I'm approximately the same height and weight as Bruce Lee was during his film career. At 5'6" in height and around 145 pounds, I have to be ferocious, so that when the star takes me out, it makes him look better, unless that actor wants the audience to believe he's invincible and that nobody can touch him. But that's not human; it's not real. The best fighters in the world get hit. Muhammad Ali was hit hundreds, if not thousands, of times over the course of his career, including being knocked down. Mike Tyson was knocked out by a relatively unknown Buster Douglas, and I was knocked down by Okao.

The stark reality is that even the greatest fighters can be hit. This is what makes Jackie Chan so real—he gets hit like a human being, and then ultimately at the end of the movie his strength overcomes his adversary and he proves victorious. When Jackie Chan's career began to take off in the early 1980s, I felt that the reality of his fight sequences would help martial artists who work in the movie business do what we love doing.

When I choreograph a fight sequence, in order for it to make sense, I have to envision the director's vision from his point of view. I also need to see the actor's vision from his point of view, which tells me what kind of energy he's putting into it.

Choreographing a fight sequence on the set of *The Price of Glory*

ABOVE: With Patrick Swayze on the film *Road House;* BELOW: With Jean-Claude Van Damme on the film *Street Fighter*

Some stunt coordinators don't follow the script's story. When I teach stunt work, I tell my students to follow the story and not to just put in a fancy kick or punch because when the audience is pulled away from the storyline by some fancy razzle-dazzle, they lose interest. The second important aspect that I teach my students is that the best way to hold a viewer's interest is to capture their emotions; that is, get the viewer emotionally involved by bringing them into the story, which can't be done by inserting fancy kicks and punches.

Over the course of many years, I've trained hundreds of actors, including Tom Cruise, Nicole Kidman, John Cusack, Nicolas Cage, Jean-Claude Van Damme, Jimmy Smits, Chuck Norris, Kurt Russell, Mark Wahberg, Louis Gossett Jr., Michelle Pfeiffer, Juliette Lewis, Michael Keaton, Woody Harrelson, Rene Russo, and Patrick Swayze.

With Van Halen's David Lee Roth and Sara

David Lee Roth of the group "Van Halen" trained with me for years. I'm flattered that the group's hit song "Jump" was inspired by me and my teaching, as noted by the opening lyrics, "I get up, and nothing gets me down / You got it tough. I've seen the toughest around / And I know, baby, just how you feel / You've got to roll with the punches to get to what's real." A week after "Jump" went Gold, David Lee Roth appeared one night on my doorstep and gifted me with the group's gold record plaque.

Before I start preparing an actor for a fight sequence, I look into their eyes and say, "Tell me what you can and cannot do. Tell me your strong points and your weak points so that I can put your strong points on camera and shy away from your weak points. I'm here to make you look good, and the only way that will happen is we need great communication, which starts by your telling me what you can get away with. In a flash, your eyes will tell me whether you're happy, mad, glad, or sad; your facial expression will tell me what you're feeling; your body movement will tell me your experience. You won't be able to hide anything from me. So let's have a truthful relationship right up front, nothing under the table, and I promise you I'll bring the best out of you and make you proud."

Since I was five years old boxing kids at the Olympic Auditorium, I've learned that I have a natural talent that allows me not only the ability to readily pick up most anything, but also to teach it. Everyone has unique gifts that they bring with them into the world, and the ability to teach is one of mine. Over the past five decades of martial arts study, I've been awarded eight black belts in as many different systems and styles.

There have been times when I've worked with actors who were having difficulty performing a fight sequence that I'd choreographed. Upon realizing the problem had to do with the actor's inner spirit and not his physical ability, I'd get into his head and instill in him the mindset and emotions of a highly proficient, lethal street fighter. Once that was in place, the actor got through the fight sequence magnificently in one take. In the film industry,

I gained a reputation for wearing many hats for one paycheck. I could train actors, teach them how to picture fight, coordinate stunts, physically get actors in shape, keep everyone safe through car hits and fire burns, as well as do second unit directing.

As I approached the mid-1990s, I was so into the movie industry that I hadn't fought for almost four years. Whenever I'd have a window of down time from a film, promoters would come to me and begin the preliminary stages of putting together a championship fight, and then I'd be contacted by a producer, and the next thing I knew I was on a plane heading for a film location. After another year of this, the kickboxing associations that sanctioned belt titles subtly suggested to me that if I wanted to keep my title, I needed to give serious thought to defending it.

EIGHT

My Last Fight— East Meets West

▼　▼　▼　▼

I n the summer of 1994, I returned from Thailand where I'd been working on the movie *Street Fighter*. During the long plane flight home, I found myself thinking about what those people on the kickboxing sanctioning committees had said. A few days later when I saw Blinky at the Jet Center, I told him that I wanted to return to the ring and asked him to find the strongest opponent out there in my category and weight division.

I could tell by the look on Blinky's face that he had his concerns. "But you haven't fought for a long time. Maybe it's better that you work up to the big fight?"

"Thanks for your concern, but I'm fighting the best or I'm not fighting."

Blinky went to work and two weeks later told me that a Japanese kickboxer named Yoshihisa Tagami had agreed to fight me. At 25 years of age, Tagami was 17 years my junior and undefeated. Since beginning his martial arts career at age 9, he'd fought 100 matches. He was known for his left lead leg roundhouse kick, won his last fight by knockout, and was Japan's current World Welterweight Champion. In Japan, Yoshihisa Tagami worked as a physical education teacher and was in excellent physical condition.

When Blinky and my managers asked if I wanted to watch tapes of Tagami's recent fights, I said that I wasn't interested. All that mattered was that Tagami was the best. The fight was on. I'd be moving up in weight, which meant that this fight would be my fifth point category and my sixth title fight in my sixth weight category. Tagami would be moving down from 170 to 154 pounds, his ideal weight for defending his title. Although I refused to verbally say this was my last fight (no champion does), deep down I knew this would in all likelihood be my last hoorah, and I was determined to be remembered by future generations of fighters as an undefeated champion.

This was the first time that the owners of Las Vegas's Mirage Hotel allowed fighters to fight there. The event promised to be a guaranteed sellout when Blinky brought in five other kickboxing world title holders—all our managed fighters—to fight that night on the same ticket. At that time, having five championship title matches on the same card was unheard of. Because this was being promoted as "The Jet's Final Fight," Blinky sold the television broadcast and pay-per-view rights to SHOWTIME.

Two hundred and seventy miles away in Las Vegas, the Mirage Hotel publicity department launched an aggressive and widespread advertising campaign. "Coming December 4th – World Championship Fight – First Time Ever!" the battle of champions was being billed as the biggest kickboxing card in world kickboxing history. Within a week, hotels throughout Las Vegas began selling out as word spread that "The Jet" was coming to wield his axe in Sin City.

As Japan's powerhouse kickboxer Yoshihisa Tagami and his entourage took to the mountains to embark on a grueling schedule of hardcore training, I began running with Maker at 4:30 in the morning. Realizing that I was about to face the toughest opponent of my career, I needed to break the energies from the Hollywood film industry, my friends and students, and the media.

The only bond I kept intact were with my wife and some members of my immediate family.

After two weeks of isolated running and light weight training, I was told by Blinky that it was time to travel to the mountaintop. Along with the four other fighters and our trainers, we sojourned to Big Bear City (different from Big Bear Lake) because its high altitude of nearly 10,000 feet had a positive effect on the blood's oxygen transport system. Over the years, Big Bear Lake was often the location of the training camps for many boxers and MMA combatants such as Oscar De La Hoya, Shane Mosley, and Tito Ortiz.

The temperature had fallen below freezing and snow had begun to fall when we arrived in Big Bear City and moved into a group of mountain cabins. Nearby was a restaurant that was open 24-hours and provided us with anything we wanted to eat. Adjacent to the restaurant was a small gym and a boxing ring that had seen considerable use over two decades. The entire area was isolated from all the lower energies.

It was early November and still dark in the early morning hours. We'd awaken, don our thick, hooded sweats and track shoes and jog for several hours in two feet of snow. Following a shower and high carb / high protein breakfast, we spent the morning training with weights and extensive bag work. After lunch, we'd get down to serious business sparring in the ring.

After spending two weeks sparring the other fighters and being careful that no one got injured, I told my trainers that I needed more intense sparring sessions. They brought in a hard-hitting champion who not only could take a beating but could also dish one out.

One afternoon during a sparring session, we got carried away and this guy started pressing me. After several solid exchanges, I could tell from the look in his eyes and his body language that something had snapped. Moments later, he came after me, swinging a barrage of knockout punches. Suddenly, at the blink of an eye it was open season on my head. Aware that my sparring partner had turned ballistic, I ducked under one of his blistering right hooks, slammed a body shot into his liver, and then nearly tore his head off with a left hook. He hit the canvas, barely conscious.

The storm had passed. The guy struggled to his feet and stood on wobbly legs and apologized for getting too heavy. I smiled and told him to forget about it, then gestured to my trainer to join me in a nearby room. Moments later when my trainer entered the room, I told him to close the door and get my left glove off. He could tell that I was in considerable pain. When my glove was removed, it was clear that my hand was swollen. It felt like it was broken, no doubt from the left hook I'd delivered minutes earlier to the head of my sparring partner.

Because there was no medical clinic close to the cabins, my trainer drove me down the hill to a physician who ordered a series of X-rays and an MRI. A half hour later, the radiology reports came in—I had a hairline fracture of my left hand. This was a potential disaster because I'm a lefty, and my left hook had always been my money shot. I told my trainer to keep this confidential. Not even my wife or any of my family were to know. A fractured hand wasn't going to stop this fight. I'd fought with far worse in the street. The doctor gave me a cortisone injection, and I planned to have another upon my arrival in Las Vegas.

Two days before the fight, I arrived at the Mirage Hotel with the other four fighters and our trainers. Thankfully, the swelling in my left hand had subsided appreciably, although my fingers were numb. After being installed in my suite and enjoying a pleasant reunion with my wife and daughter, I went to another room in the hotel where I was greeted by members of the Blackfoot Piegan Nation —Chief Willy Big Bull, Chief White Rainbow, and a tribal woman named Ona—who had traveled from Canada with my headdress, vest, and pants to perform a sacred Native American ceremony before my fight.

Years earlier, Chief Willy Big Bull had given me the name Thundering Iron Horse—Thunder because my strikes have the power of thunder, Iron because my body is like steel, and Horse

Elsa (Blackfoot Medicine woman who gave Sara her Native American name Eaglewoman), Sara, and Chief Willy Big Bull

ABOVE: My warrior's headdress of the Blackfoot Nation; BELOW: My sacred pipe and its leather pouch. The black pouch holds sacred tobacco

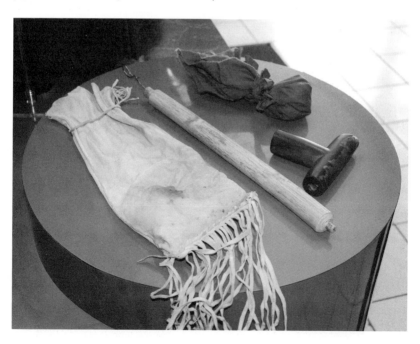

because as a warrior I'm like a workhorse that never stops and because I'm fast as a horse.

Later that afternoon, the four of us drove to an isolated place in the desert where Willy Big Bull had earlier erected a sacred circle that surrounded a stone altar. After sage and sweet grass were burned to attract the spirits of our ancestors, we smoked the ceremonial sacred pipe, the smoke from which carried our prayers up to the creator.

As the sun began to set, White Rainbow sang the warrior's song to Ono's drum beating, and Willy Big Bull presented me with my headdress of sacred eagle feathers and my beaded pants and vest. Sometime later as the ceremony drew to an end, I was in the zone, my soul having traveled upwards to a place where it looked down at the two Blackfoot chiefs and Ono who had begun to disassemble our sacred ceremonial place.

That night, the fight was held in the Grand Ballroom of the Mirage Hotel and was billed as the biggest-ever such event in the United States. Among the sold out crowd of 3,600 spectators that included a crush of celebrities were hundreds of Japanese who had flown to Las Vegas from Japan to root for Japan's last hope of beating "The Jet" and taking the belt back to their home country. In addition, fans came from Canada, Australia, England, Jerusalem, and Africa. Las Vegas hotels had been sold out for weeks, as the Mirage Hotel became ground zero for a championship fight that to the kickboxing world was on a par with a fight between Muhammad Ali and Joe Frazier.

Cecil Peoples acted as referee, Chuck Norris and Don "The Dragon" Wilson were ringside commentators for SHOWTIME, and the ring announcer was Jimmy Lennon, Jr. In my corner were my three trainers Stan Ward, Jeff Mulvin, and Hector Lopez. At ringside, my brother Arnold, his eyes riveted on the ring, sat beside my trainers.

When Yoshihisa Tagami and I met in the center of the ring to fight for the WKA Light middleweight Championship, I could tell by the intensity in his eyes and his posture that he had trained exceptionally hard. He appeared alert and empowered with the energy of ten samurai warriors. Out of respect for his country, he had his head shaved in a buzz cut that featured a large "J" on the back of his head flanked by two lightning bolts. Although I was as empowered and ready for this fight as Tagami, I was concerned about my injured left hand that a half hour earlier I'd smeared with Ben-Gay and wrapped tightly in my glove. Further injuring my hand was one thing. Wondering how long it might take my opponent to catch on to my injury was a far greater concern. If he did, and being the smart fighter that he was, I had no doubt that he would capitalize on this in a big hurry.

After the referee gave us final instructions in the middle of the ring, I returned to my corner and waited for the bell for round one. Moments after the bell rang, I was suddenly in the middle of the ring slugging it out with Japan's champion Yoshihisa Tagami and hearing my brother yelling, "You can do this, brother!" Halfway through the round, I could sense that Tagami had tremendous energy reserves and that I was in for a fight. I'd asked for the best there was, and that's exactly what I got.

All of a sudden, Tagami came after me, and I remember getting hit hard and thinking *this guy's fast and he's got power!* Seemingly from out of nowhere, I smelled the strong scent of sage and sweet grass as I felt my soul rise. Seconds later, I was looking down at the ring and watching me fighting Tagami. When the bell rang, I watched myself sitting down on my stool and being surrounded by my corner men. I could see them talking to me but had no idea what they were saying. I heard their muffled voices as if I were underwater. Suddenly, their nearly inaudible voices were replaced by the loud yelling of nearly 4,000 fans. It was as if I'd suddenly gone from a peaceful walk in the country to stepping into a jet turbine engine. I kept going in and out of my body, thinking *what is happening to me? Was Tagami hit me so hard that I'm suffering from a concussion?*

The next six rounds amounted to a real rock 'em, sock 'em fight. Tagami would come at me with a flurry of punches and

My fight with Yoshihisa Tagami

kicks, then I'd take out my axe and chase him across the ring with my own onslaught. The fight was as close as a fight can get. I knew both corners had to be concerned about the point totals and were hoping their fighter would land a knockdown blow, or better yet a knockout. Several times I had Tagami hurt, but I couldn't put him down without my left hand that by the end of the third round was numb and throbbing.

There was no question that my opponent was fighting with the same unyielding determination as I was, and I wondered if he was tapping into the strength of the samurai as I had tapped into the strength of the Blackfoot and Apache nations. One things was for certain, and that was we were both pulling out all the stops.

All of a sudden, BOOM! I got hit with a solid punch that sent my body crashing to the canvas. It was the second time in my career that I'd been knocked down. I saw the canvas approaching me in slow motion and could read the minds of the thousands of fans who were no doubt thinking *The Jet is hurt and finished.*

Then all of a sudden, I'm back up and on the attack again. Everything kicked in—my father's beatings, my years of street fighting and martial arts training, my mother's voice telling me over and over that I am the chosen one who will plant the Urquidez flag. Again I went on the attack and had Tagami dazed, but without my left hook, I couldn't put him away. After the third round, the few times I used my left hand, the pain had shot all the way up my arm and into my brain. As I watched Tagami recover, I again was coming in and out of my body and wasn't hearing anything. I was in a different world. I wasn't spiritually grounded, I was spiritually high. Tagami was hitting me, and I didn't feel anything, except for the pain in my left hand.

In the tenth round, I came back into my body and suddenly heard people howling and screaming, and yet at the same time I could hear Tagami's heartbeat. I knew it was his heartbeat and not my own because its sound got louder as he came closer, and quieter when he moved away.

I kept hitting him and scoring points. Again, I had him hurt, this time seriously, but I couldn't finish him because my left hand—my money shot—was practically useless. I heard my brother screaming, "Left hook 'em! Finish him!" Tagami had begun limping, and I knew that I had finally managed to inflict severe injuries to his legs.

In twelfth and final round I got a second wind. I went after Tagami with everything I had left in the tank, but he was too determined. I could see in his eyes that this brave and courageous warrior was fighting for his country and was probably willing to die trying to defeat me. After the bell rang ending the fight, we hugged each other. The crowd was on its feet, cheering for both fighters. They had truly gotten their money's worth. For me, the premonition I'd had a month earlier that this was to be the toughest fight of my career turned out to be true.

Victory!

Minutes later, the entire assemblage inside the Grand Ballroom of the Mirage Hotel stood in silence as the ring announcer walked to the center of the ring and delivered the decision that was handed down by neutral, veteran, world-class judges in Las Vegas: former WKA world champion Fred Royers of Netherlands, WKA women's champion Dayle Baykey of Canada, and a Nevada Athletic Commission regular. After what felt like an eternity, someone beside me raised my arms as the announcer said, "The winner . . . and STILL undefeated—" and I looked at Tagami, who smiled, and then got on his knees and cried as he began bowing to me. In Japan, the bow is a timeless sign of respect and admiration, not a display of subservience as it is sometimes mistaken in the west.

After the fight, I addressed the sports media and told the reporters that I wanted everyone to remember this fight as a contest between two champion gladiators and that because of Tagami's performance that night, he should return to Japan as a hero.

Following the press conference, Sara and I went to my post-fight celebration party. I learned the following morning that Tagami had come to the party just minutes after Sara and I left, bandaged and walking on crutches. As hurt as he was, he'd come to publicly congratulate me. In my absence, he told everyone through his interpreter that it had been an honor to fight me and that he will never forget it. There was so much emotion generated by that fight that a year later people were still talking about it as if it had occurred the night before.

After Sara and I left the celebration party, we went dancing at Sharkey's. Coincidentally, this night, December 4th, was her birthday. Nearly 25 years had passed since I first saw her walking down the street in the Valley sporting a long mane of hair. I had put her through a lot. Most women wouldn't have had the courage, strength, and endurance to do what she did to be with me. Back then I wasn't an easy person to be with. Now I am because now everybody gets to mess with me.

After returning from Las Vegas, life gradually returned to nor-

Sara's Uncle Domingo

mal as I refocused my attention and energy on my film career, the Jet Center, and my stable of fighters. Then at 4:31 in the morning on January 17, 1994 the north-central region of the San Fernando Valley was hit with a massive earthquake that lasted about 15 seconds. While the earthquake had a strong 6.7 seismic reading, its ground acceleration was one of the highest ever instrumentally recorded in North America.

The Jet Center was practically a stone's throw from the epicenter of the Northridge earthquake. Although the quake had inflicted damage to the building, it wasn't severe enough to result in the fire marshals red-tagging the structure as unsafe for occupancy. As things turned out, however, this amounted to merely a stay of execution. The damage that the earthquake had caused was primarily to the building's roof, and when heavy rains fell in December, the entire Jet Center was flooded. Because of the extensive damage, we were forced to close our doors for good. It

My 105-year-old grandmother Delores Rosa

had been a sensational ride. We had remained open for 13 wonderful and highly productive years.

With the Jet Center now in our past, Sara and I spent much of our newfound free time continuing our study of spirituality. To me, learning about the full nature of my spirituality is crucial to my core because without this foundation, I am merely guessing.

Throughout the next year, Sara's Uncle Domingo continued teaching her their Native American ways. He would come to our home and spend hours with Sara, teaching her through ancient tribal stories. During this same timeframe, my grandmother, who was 105 years of age, would tell Sara and me stories about how she rode alongside Poncho Villa, the prominent general during the Mexican Revolution.

Sara was truly tuned into my grandmother Delores Rosa who had extraordinary wisdom and experience. Between Sara's Uncle

Traveling with Sara and Monique

Domingo and my grandmother, Sara and I learned a great deal from their teachings. Both told their stories with such intensity that as a listener it was almost like stepping into the story, itself, and becoming an integral part of it.

During this time I spent with Sara, I finally realized that she is my soul mate, my twin flame, and my equal on this earth—and all of my accomplishments in life mean nothing compared to the love and bond that I have with Sara, my daughter Monique, and my grandson Levi.

NINE

The Jet's Gym
and The Breakfast Club

▼   ▼   ▼   ▼

After the Jet Center closed, I needed a place to open another training facility, although finding a building that
was comparable to the Jet Center wasn't going to be
easy. Meanwhile, there was a guy in North Hollywood who ran a
small gym. He invited me to workout at his place, and I accepted
because I needed to stay in shape. I'd go early in the morning
and hit the bags and skip rope. After a while, my students learned
where I was training and followed me there. Before long I was
using the gym to teach my students, so I started giving money to
the owner. When a few months later he grew tired of running the
place, he offered it to me, and I took over his lease.

A year later on April 1, 1995, I officially opened the Jet's Gym.
The commercial building housed my dojo in front and a tanning
salon in back. The setup was awkward because my students had
to walk through the tanning salon in order to get to my dojo. En
route, the guys were distracted by the women walking around in
skimpy bikinis. Ladies who wanted a full tan wore even less, just
nipple cups and a G-string. When I tried to explain to the salon's

Working on building the "Jet's Gym"

owner that her salon was in a fighting gym and that her customers were distracting my fighters, she replied, "No, *I'm* in a salon. *You're* in the fighting gym." Weeks went on in this manner, and we were getting nowhere. Finally, Sara said that the arrangement wasn't good for my students—and it especially wasn't good for the school's reputation.

Thankfully, the people next door wanted out of their lease. Their place was much larger, which was great because the Jet's Gym was growing rapidly. An added advantage was that it was adjacent to a Gold's Gym, which was fertile ground for new students. I signed a new lease and went to work on my customary remodel that included the addition of showers and a row of bleachers in the front lobby where visitors could watch students fighting in the ring. Because Sara didn't have a place to do her healing work, I built a room for her in back that soon became very popular.

Six months into our new place, I formed the Breakfast Club,

which was a two-hour fighting class. On Saturday mornings, the weekend didn't start until *after* the Breakfast Club ended. People would drive long distances on Friday to attend class the following morning. We'd run six or seven miles at Griffith Park, return to the gym around noon, and then would suit up for battle and go to war.

After the class ended, we gathered at a nearby restaurant. It was a big place, and the owner had a private table set up for us in back. When the six-hour class ended, emotions were running high due to the intensity of the full contact fighting. Our gathering afterwards at the restaurant gave those who attended the Breakfast Club an opportunity to vent their emotions. Often I'd hear a student comment to another, "I wanted to kick your rear because after you knew I was hurt, you took advantage of me." Because their souls had been laid bare, their communications with each other was a spiritual experience. This was why I called this special Saturday morning class "The Breakfast Club" because the class fed the student's mind and body, and our meeting afterwards fed their soul.

I recall one day at the restaurant members of our group represented seven different countries. Earlier in the day, Angel and Majid fought each other and were now sitting across from me at the table. Angel said in reference to Majid, "You know, Sensei, I would never tell my family that I'm breaking bread with somebody from Pakistan. Here our two countries are at war, and my family would never understand, let alone accept, how I can sit at the same table and break bread and hug Majid."

Majid agreed. "I would never tell my mother and father, or the rest of my family, that I'm sitting with a Jew, laughing and eating with him."

Someone from Iran would speak, then another from Russia, and then soon students from many other countries would join in the conversation. The warrior's spirit has no boundaries. In a sense, the Breakfast Club drew a resemblance to the United Nations, which is why the United Nations flag is part of the Ukidokan patch. Many said that this international camaraderie would only happen on these Saturday mornings at the Jet's Gym.

To accommodate students who traveled great distances to attend the Breakfast Club, the gym had dormitories upstairs where students could sleep. There were no beds. People who stayed over slept in sleeping bags or on the floor wrapped in blankets. In the morning, they'd come downstairs and shower before heading out for our morning run at Griffith Park. There was nothing elaborate about the Jet's Gym, which was really a poor man's Jet Center. Students were there only for training.

The Jet's Gym had no age restrictions. I trained students from 15 to 75 years of age. One of my students was called "The General." He was 65 and would step into the ring and fight students 30 and 40 years his junior. I made sure that he never felt threatened. Everyone knew that if they purposely hurt The General or injured him through carelessness, I'd jump in the ring and get busy.

Everyone was welcome, regardless of what experience or inexperience they brought with them. It wasn't uncommon to see two grandmothers sparring in ring at the Breakfast Club.

Whenever I started a new group, I'd ask how many were attending for their first time. Several would raise their hand. Then I'd ask how many fought professionally for a living. Most raised their hand. The remainder were looky-loos who had signed up because they wanted to see what the Breakfast Club was like, and a few others who had come to test themselves. The point is that people came from many different background to satisfy a variety of needs.

Following my prep talk, I ran them through a series of stretching exercises and then told them to put on their gear. With everyone now suited up for sparring, I'd get into the internal. The key was to amp up their emotions by placing them in a threatening environment that was unpredictable because it would be constantly changing.

I could see their anxiety level increase the moment I began explaining what they'd be facing. "Everybody is going to fight everybody. So if you see someone in this gym that you wouldn't want to fight, you're going to fight that person today. I'm going to teach you techniques outside the ring, but when I switch you, you'll go into the ring and fight. Then when you come out of the ring, you'll do techniques and work with people who will try to hurt you and touch all your fear buttons. After you've trained with them for a while, you'll go back into the ring and fight someone else. You'll continue doing this for a couple hours, and after you've fought eight to ten opponents, you'll know the emotional aspect of what the street feels like when you're in a fight for your life."

This type of realistic training evoked a tidal wave of emotion. The square jungle, which I call the ring, touches every part of a person's life. Behind the closed doors of the Jet's Gym, everything came up because these people felt threatened, and they got a chance to see it, to feel it, and to consciously dispel it by summoning up the courage to take action. This inner battle of emotion was clearly apparent in their eyes and their facial expressions. This unique training at the Jet's Gym on Saturday mornings was what became known throughout the world as the Breakfast Club.

▼ ▼ ▼ ▼

For the next several years, life was good. The Jet's Gym was filling up, and I was spending much of my time doing what I love best—teaching. Sara and I were happier than we'd ever been, and I was enjoying the one aspect of life that my mother placed the most importance—familia. It seemed that Maker had aligned all the stars and planets in my favor.

On March 1, 2003 my father passed away at the ripe old age of 91 years. He had led a long and full life. Even though we'd had a checkered past, in his later years we were able to mend a few fences and build a bridge between us that allowed us to come together. His gravestone said it all—"Beloved Father, Grandfather, Great Grandfather Moving to the Rhythm." I'd like to believe

LEFT: One of my greatest teachers, my father, in his later years; BELOW: Grandpa with Levi

that he died knowing that he'd made a contribution to my success as a fighter, even if it was only a matter of my desire to make him proud of me. Perhaps he lived out his dream to become a great fighter vicariously through me.

A year later on February 4, 2004, my daughter Monique gave birth to a son whom she named Levi. His birth has been a true joy in my life because, as is the case with many grandfathers, Levi's birth has given me the opportunity to make up for the mistakes I made as a father. A day doesn't pass that Levi isn't Sara and my main focus. He truly continues to be a blessing in our lives.

Monique and Levi

Then just when things were running smoothly, Maker handed me a series of painful lessons that began on the spring of 2006
when my brother Ruben became critically ill. He had sugar di-
abetes and sorrowfully went blind. I'd always envisioned Ruben
as a powerful warrior. At the time he became terminally ill, I'd
returned to filmmaking and was in Bulgaria with John Cusak
filming *The Contract*. Arnold called and told me that Ruben was

My brother Ruben

on his death bed and that I wouldn't make it back before he passed. Arnold felt that it made more sense that I stay in Bulgaria and finish the movie, which I did. In my absence, my family buried Ruben. A week later when I returned, I went to Ruben's gravesite and tearfully paid my respects.

▼   ▼   ▼   ▼

Six months later on January 10, 2007, four dozen people were waiting for me to teach the Breakfast Club, but I never arrived. Instead, I called Sensei Jeff Mulvin and told him that I was en route to a hospital to join my family.

Days earlier, I was out of the country on a film location when Arnold called to tell me that my sister Lilly had been hospitalized and was in a coma. Two years earlier, she'd been diagnosed with a life-threatening illness and elected to not tell anyone. She literally hid her illness from everyone and refused all conventional methods of treatment. As was the case with Ruben, I'd always envisioned Lilly as a powerful warrior. She'd been so strong that she felt she could triumph over her illness, as she had in the ring and many other areas throughout her life.

I raced to the hospital where I joined Lilly's husband Blinky and other members of our family. Sitting on her bed, I took Lilly's hand and pleaded with her, "C'mon, Sis, you're strong. You've got too much fight in you and still much to do here." It was hard for me to see her in such a weakened state because I'd always known her to be a powerful and strong warrior, even when I was a kid. Since my father left when I was eight years old, Lilly had helped fill a tremendous void. We'd always been so connected, I can't describe the unfathomable emotional pain I felt when she told me that she wanted to be with Momma. In keeping with her totally unselfish nature, she looked up at me and said, "I'm so sorry that you have to see me like this." Even as her life was coming to end, her primary concern was with others.

When I left Lilly's room, I walked down the hall and hid be-

My beautiful sister Lilly. I miss her more with each passing day

hind a janitor's cart. I wanted to disappear. Within moments, the dam broke and I cried harder than I thought anyone could. My crying intensified to wailing as layer by layer I brought years of emotional pain forward. No one in my family—or anyone else for that matter—had ever heard me cry the way I did that day. My sobs were pleas of "Don't leave, don't go!" My words weren't so much *don't leave me* as they were *don't leave, don't go, you're not ready to go, I love you so much.* For 55 years of my life, I had allowed myself to love so few people—and now two of them, my mother and Lilly—were gone.

Around that same timeframe, my landlord had given me 30 days to vacate the Jet's Gym, and three weeks of those 30 days had already elapsed by the time I arrived home from being on location. Apparently, no one in my family wanted to burden me with this bad news from my landlord. When I was finally informed, I didn't care. Lilly was astronomically more important, and after she passed, I just wanted to be alone. I told my black belts to take the trophies, my championship belts, and a few other personal items, and to leave the rest, including the ring.

Days later, I drove to San Fernando Mission Cemetery where, by now, I was no stranger. Having spent 56 years as a member of the strong and vibrant Urquidez clan, standing in that cemetery and looking down at the side-by-side gravestones of my mother, Ruben, and Lilly was a major blow to my spirit.

Then within a year, I lost my brother Mando, who died from full organ shutdown. After losing my mother in 1992, followed by the losses of Ruben, Lilly, and Mando within a three year period, I understood what actor Marlon Brando felt when he said, "The messenger of misery has visited my house." Throughout my life, my mother had instilled in me the importance of familia, and now I was left with the cold reality that the Urquidez clan had lost four of its key members.

As hard as I fought it, darkness and depression came over me, and I began to lose interest in practically everything. Over the course of several weeks, I became angry. I had a new slant on the

At San Fernando Mission Cemetery to honor my family members

world, which was that it lacked an acceptable amount of truth. With my gift of deep intuition now at an all-time high, I began to see red flags waving over the heads of practically everyone I came in contact with. Often with little tact, I pulled their sheets from them and mirrored their truths. I had zero tolerance for lies. I'd say to people, including family members, "Why don't you be truthful with yourself? What are you afraid of? Why don't you just come out and say what's really on your mind?"

Some would shut me off, few would become belligerent, but most would just dodge me when they saw me coming. Ironically, I'd become the type of truth seeker that Sara was when I first met her. Back then, when Sara used to demand that people be truthful and open, it annoyed me to no end, and I'd stand up to her. Now, however, I had no objection to what I was doing—although she did.

Sara would tell me that I had to calm down and that there was an easier, softer way to get people to face their truth. I'd tell her that there is no greater power on Earth than the pure unadulterated truth and that people needed to live that way. She would tell me that the truth I was bringing up was scary and painful to people, and that these people I was confronting weren't ready to hear the truth. Unfazed, I'd reply, "They have to learn it sooner or later."

Then one day Sara laid it on the line and asked, "Who do you think you are that you feel it's your responsibility to tell them the truth? Do you really feel that you have the right to throw it in their face regardless of whether or not they like it?"

I've often said that Sara is my challenger, and this was a prime example. She was right. I was the one who had been in my own internal warfare and was taking out my frustration on others. In reality, I'd become angry because of the loss of my mother, Ruben, Lilly, and Mando. More importantly, I was angered that Lilly hadn't been honest with me and told me of her illness. I became angry with Ruben because he hadn't told me that he was sick, and I was angry with Arnold because he didn't tell me about Ruben until it was too late for me to be at Ruben's bedside when he passed. That no one had told me about my lease being terminated on the Jet's Gym added to my anger. Somehow I decided that if my family wasn't going to be truthful with me, I was going to get the truth out of everybody else.

Days later, the real crux of the matter hit me when I realized that the reason Lilly hadn't told me about her illness was because she didn't want to burden me with it, and instead, wanted me to stay focused. The same held true with the others. No one wanted to upset me. And then I recognized that what I was really angry about was that I felt that my family thought I needed to be sheltered. While it was true that throughout my life I was the baby of the family and that my mother and Lilly had protected me from many woes, in my mind I'd long since undergone the rite of passage. I'd become a responsible person. Because of my hard work, I'd opened many doors for people, including my own family. In addition, I'd physically fought the toughest men in the world, as well as my own internal demons, and had been victorious. I'd become a loving father, husband, grandfather, and provider and I felt that I deserved to be treated as an adult. God knows I'd earned it. Through Sara's help, once I reached that understanding, I got comfortable, and my internal warfare—as well as the storm it had created—subsided.

From that moment and to this day, I've kept my mother and father, Lilly, Ruben, and Mando alive through their stories. There are times when I can actually see and hear them. Although they died in the flesh, their spirits live in my heart. I often talk with my mom and think about the many wonderful things she told me throughout her lifetime. Sara will see me smiling and ask what I'm smiling about, and I'll tell her that I'm just remembering something my mom had said. There are other times when I'll suddenly be laughing, and Sara will ask, "What are you laughing about? Let me in on it." Then I'll share with her whatever it is and she'll break out laughing with me. What a beautiful gift Maker has given all of us—the ability to remember our most precious moments.

Because Ruben, Lilly, and Mando were such an active part of the fighting Urquidez clan, I also keep them alive through my sport. As 2008 drew to a close, their memories inspired me to take time off from making movies and get back into the martial arts in order to fulfill what I now know is my purpose in life, which is to teach.

Over a span of nearly four decades, the sport of kickboxing in America has undergone great change. In the 1970s the true warriors fought. Then in the 1980s the sport began to change, particularly in the latter part of the decade when the majority of the earlier kickboxing legends and heroes were disappearing, along with the kickboxing associations that were organized in the late 1970s and 1980s. For nearly two decades, I fought in every major league there was. I outlasted every one of them. I took their belts—one day they're here, the next year they're gone. Another league would start up. I took their title, and then they'd be gone. When I stopped fighting, I held every title—six titles in five weight divisions—WKA, NKL, PKA, and Muay Thai.

As the sport moved into the 1990s, a new breed of fighters emerged that, because they had no heroes to follow, created their own. Suddenly, everyone was a world champion through their own newly-formed league. Most became performers instead of fighters, their main interest being how much money they would be paid. Most either lost or never had a passion for the sport of full contact karate. I needed to find a way to bring back the Bushido heart—or the internal aspect of the martial art—to kickboxing.

UKIDOKAN...

U represents the family Urquidez.

KI represents the spirit or natural power.

DO is the Way of the path. It denotes a discipline and philosophy with moral and spiritual connotations, the ultimate aim being enlightenment and personal development. A practitioner of the Way is known as a "master of Strategy."

KAN respresents the house, the house of Urquidez

UKIDOKAN!

TEN

Ukidokan

Following the closure of the Jet's Gym and the burials of my family members, I was without a dojo. Looking back, I realize that this was the way it was meant to be, for I needed time to connect with my inner being—time that ultimately was spent reformulating my art. For a long while, I wandered like a Samurai who roamed the countryside in Feudal Japan, a lone figure and his sword owing allegiance to no one but himself.

In coming to further understand Bushido, or the Way of the Warrior, I recognized that the understanding of a physical attack isn't so much about the attack, itself, but how one perceives it. How do you feel about it? Not how do you feel about the punch, kick, throw, or being choked out—the physical action—but how do you feel about the fact that there is a person, an energy, a spirit or soul that is trying to inflict harm on your physical being? This is the *emotional* element of the attack being directed at you, and it has a vibration that connects to you, often in a negative way.

The physical training of learning how to evade a punch or kick, countering a throw, or slipping out of a chokehold is twofold—one, knowledge, and two, the physical application that includes everything from subtleties to brute force. In my time alone, during which I did considerable soul searching and reflection, I recognized that "now" training is the internal training, specifically the understanding of it. This internal training is what I'm teaching today. The warrior within—bring it out and let's see how it *feels* and what you're doing with it.

There is a great story that illustrates this. The two participants are Dan Inosanto and Bruce Lee. Years ago when Dan began training with Bruce, Dan was hitting a focus pad that Bruce held in his hand at face level. Bruce called out, "Hit!" and Dan punched the glove. They kept doing this, and although Dan was punching with fairly good speed and power, Bruce wasn't satisfied and didn't feel that Dan was doing his best. Lowering the glove to his side, Bruce walked up to Dan and, without a word, slapped him hard in the face, then quickly stepped back, held up the glove, and yelled, "Now hit!" In a flash, Dan hit the glove so hard that he nearly ripped it from Bruce's hand. Bruce beamed. "Ah! Now you're hitting with emotional content!"

After many decades of studying, training, and teaching the martial arts, I've come to believe that a true master is one who understands the emotional psyche of what both he and his student are doing. Again, I'm not talking about the physical, external aspect, but about spiritual and mental warfare, which are both internal.

In addressing the internal, I've re-developed a Free Form martial arts by combining nine different styles to create my system that I call Ukidokan, which means "Way of Life" or, as it is commonly referred to, Internal Training. Further translated, this way of life is a means to control your emotions when under pressure through applying techniques that work under pressure. This internal part—the Bushido Way—is what most people aren't getting in their training. The internal—meaning inside-out instead of outside-in—is the difference because the internal is the source of your strength and understanding.

Early on, there was a division among my family. Arnold, Mando, Ruben, and Lilly were drawn to the hard, angular style of Shotokan. In contrast, I was drawn to the Chinese, circular styles of White Crane Kung-fu, Lima Lama, Judo, and Kenpo Karate.

Over time, we came together in the middle of the road, as it were, to form a system that combined both hard and soft styles. Not knowing what to call it, we simply called it Kenpo-Shotokan. When we first put it together, people would ask, "Are you Kenpo or are you Shotokan?" The reality was we weren't entirely one or the other. Today, what we had combined would be referred to as mixed martial arts. Back then, to us it was simply the way we fought.

Prior to my defeating Japan's champions, the Japanese had never seen my type of fighting. Not long after I defeated their champions, they began asking what I called it. When I told them Kenpo-Shotokan, they replied, "No. You have to be one or the other. Whatever you're doing, you have to name it so that we know what it is and how to rate it."

As my popularity in Japan soared, Japanese businessmen wanted to open a mother school in Japan based on what I do; and from that mother school they intended to open a chain of schools throughout Japan. Although the basic system of Japanese kickboxing was relatively simple and clear-cut, American kickboxing didn't have a standard curriculum. Of course, without a curriculum that could be taught to thousands of students and be used as the standard for awarding belt ranks, it would be impossible to certify instructors, let alone masters. This was essentially the same problem that Bruce Lee encountered a decade earlier when people were insisting that he clearly define his art and that he establish a standard curriculum.

In much the same way, and for the same reasons that Bruce finally elected to more clearly define his art of Jeet Kune Do, I, too, put my mind to work to resolve the dilemma, and over a period of five years developed my system of kickboxing, which I call Ukidokan. *U* is for my last name, *Ki* is for the internal, and *Kan* is for the place. I took the best from each other the basic nine styles that I was taught and re-glazed and modified it so that it worked extremely well under pressure—and it works for everyone from hardhat construction workers to relatively inactive people who work desk jobs.

What I teach today is a combination of many styles. My kicks are Tae Kwon Do, which is a Korean style; my throwing is judo, aikido, and jujitsu, which individually and working in combination make up my ground game; my hands are trapping and rooted in Kenpo; my outside movement is from White Crane Kung-fu; my clenches are Lima Lama; my dancing footwork and hand movements are western boxing; and my wrestling moves came from my mother. All of these disciplines come together in Ukidokan as a way of life because my art deals with the inner emotions of all types of warfare—physical, mental, spiritual, and character. And again, the vast majority of warfare situations that most people face during a single day or throughout their lifetime are not physical.

After naming my system, I created a curriculum for sets of ranking. In Ukidokan Karate, there are ten levels of proficiency: white belt, yellow belt, orange belt, purple belt, blue belt, green belt, three degrees of brown belt, and then Shodan, which is the first degree of black belt. Important to note that karate is far more than getting a black belt. Although not everyone, most people train almost entirely in the physical aspect of karate, and only delve minimally, if at all, in the mental and spiritual aspects. Today's generation of martial artists feel that once they've been awarded their black belt, then they no longer have to train. Oftentimes they start off by asking how long it will take them to obtain a black belt. This is the wrong way to begin one's martial arts journey because the reality is that one's journey in martial arts is to achieve, or arrive at, an understanding of what Shodan means. The day that a student receives their black belt marks the beginning—not the ending—of their understanding their journey.

Contained in the Ukidokan Karate curriculum are a wide

assortment of techniques that defend against grabs, kicks and punches, and weapon assaults. These techniques are contained in katas, or forms, that the student uses to practice alone or with a group and are similar to what a boxer does when shadowboxing. The astute martial artist who wants to become a true master will spend considerable time perfecting the forms because the forms are what fine tunes their art.

Besides restructuring Ukidokan Karate, I developed my own system of Ukidokan Kickboxing. Instead of belt ranks, proficiency in Ukidokan Kickboxing is noted by levels. While Ukidokan Karate is an art, Ukidokan Kickboxing is a sport. Another key distinction is that in Ukidokan Karate that is practiced in the dojo, there is always someone there to intervene and stop anyone from being harmed. In Ukidokan Kickboxing there is no one to intervene. Once the match begins, the two combatants are on their own until the match is decided by decision or by knockout. Unlike Ukidokan Karate, in Ukidokan Kickboxing the student is confronted by their fear, and because of this, they have the best opportunity for personal growth.

In addition to Ukidokan's ranking systems and teaching curriculums, I created a patch. The center of the patch is symbolic of a temple. To most people, a temple is a place of worship, but to me the temple is a place where people enter into a safe haven, which is my dojo, or what the Japanese call a training hall.

The kodokan, which is a Japanese pagoda, represents a doorway to knowledge. When a student enters the dojo through this doorway, they're coming to learn far more than the self-defense art of karate—they are coming to learn about themselves.

The Ukidokan patch also has a double-headed eagle. The eagle to the right is the messenger of God. It's your prayer, your plea, and your want. The eagle to the left is the carnal eagle, the eagle (our own ego) that blinds us, the eagle that actually stops us from becoming our better selves.

And finally, the United Nations flag because my teaching is worldwide. My patch is round because my teaching is universal.

Only my black belts are given this patch. They wear it over their hearts because the patch is their shield from the outside world.

The great majority of people who take up studying the martial arts do so because they want to defend themselves against a violent physical attack. And while that's a good reason, most people—unless they live in a high crime inner city, work in law enforcement, or are in the military—who train in the martial arts, even for years and even decades, won't ever have a physical encounter. This is not to say, however, that they will walk through life without being attacked, because in reality most people come under some form of attack every day of their lives.

Besides defending against a physical attack, Ukidokan addresses other forms of attack. For example, you can be the target of verbal warfare, which can be as damaging—sometimes more so—to your mind, spirit, and overall wellbeing than a physical attack on your body. Two people are engaged in an argument. It's not a debate. They're arguing because their beliefs systems are in conflict. They each think the other is wrong and argue to the extremes. That's mental warfare and it's different from when two people are having a debate in which each is right or wrong based on facts that are presented. When people argue, emotions become involved, which means it's not a debate. They become angry because each is touching home base and hitting nerves, trigger points, and hot spots.

Warfare is more than a threat to your physical body and has a much wider scope. Warfare is anything that disrupts your inner peace. Physical warfare can include everything from someone purposely bumping into you to someone trying to stab or choke you to death. Verbal warfare can be as simple as someone confronting another for cutting in line. Oftentimes the most threatening warfare is when a person's dark spirit is aggressive. You walk into a place and soon become aware of a creepy guy staring at you from across the room. As time passes, he comes closer and his glares are increasingly menacing. You begin to feel his dark energy and a strong intuition that this person wants to rob or hurt you.

What's happening in this situation is that your spirits have entered into spiritual war. Then there's a guy who thinks he's all that. He's Rico Suave and has a cocky air about him that says, "Eh, look at me. I'm everything, man, and you're nothing." That's spiritual warfare because spiritual energy is involved.

Once a student enters the dojo, they become a "warrior of the light" because once inside the dojo, they can see clearly what is in front of them. They're taught to perceive mental energy, physical energy, spiritual energy, and character energy. The vision of their eyes gives them understanding. They're trained to identity the type of potentially harmful energy—or type of warfare—that is before them and learn how to defend against it. Eventually all of their senses begin to find the yin/yang balance, which is internal. Unfortunately, most martial artists are so heavily focused on learning their physical self-defense art that they forget that balance. In order to find a balance and understand it, one must first travel the entire pendulum, experiencing one extreme to the other.

I teach the art of war—mental warfare, physical warfare, spiritual warfare, and character warfare. All carry energies that attack you, which in my view was best understood by those who taught guerilla warfare. Back when I was a teenager, I was fascinated by the teachings of one of the great guerilla warriors, Augusto Pinochet. If I had the chance to stand face to face to talk with him, I would love to have understood his thoughts on capturing the enemy (again, when I use the word enemy, I'm talking about many different types of energy). I would love to have known how Pinochet felt about the spiritual aspect of battle and how he did it because most great warriors have this spiritual understanding.

As I talked about in an earlier chapter, during my fight with Yoshihisa Tagami at the Mirage Hotel in Las Vegas, there were times during the fight that my soul actually took flight. During those times, I had a chance to see my opponent from a different point of view or perspective. I remember when this was occurring thinking, *if I can see through three different windows, looking with the same eyes, then I can have a better understanding of the art of war, in the way I see things, and how to defeat this man.* Equally amazing was that I was in a grand ballroom among 3,600 loud spectators, and yet I could hear my opponent's heartbeat. Amazingly, the sound of all those screaming fans was silenced, but I could hear Tagami's labored breathing.

Many professional and Olympic athletes have talked about experiencing what they call "the mental edge," which is similar to the state of mind that I'm talking about. These athletes would understand how I could take my soul and travel to the opposite side of my enemy, see something that I couldn't see in front of me, then bring my soul back into my body's awareness and look through the windows of my eyes and think *there are my opponent's weaknesses that I couldn't see from where I was before, but now I can see them because I'm seeing from more than just one perspective.* If I could talk to Augusto Pinochet or other legendary guerilla warfare fighters like Ernesto Che Guevara, these are some of the things that I'd like to ask about. Did they travel like this, and how did they capture their opponents?

Over the years, many people have asked me how I became successful, not only in the ring, but in life. My definition of success isn't centered on monetary wealth and an abundance of physical possessions, although that's a relatively small part of success. Rather, the main component of a successful life is robust physical health, a satisfactory connection with the Creator who made me, and peace of mind. Three things have been instrumental in becoming a success. First is knowing where my power comes from. Second is knowing how to access it. And third, having tapped into an eternal source of power, knowing how to use that power for good.

Many years ago while conducting a large seminar of black belts, I asked those in attendance where they got their power. Some said their power came from God. I then asked them how they accessed it. Did they go to church or the temple to ask God to give them power? They weren't sure. Others said their power came from within, while still others identified their power as chi energy. When I asked how they accessed their power, one said through breath medicine. I asked what type of power they accessed, and they answered the power gave them the ability to break boards, bricks, and ice.

Realizing none were understanding what I was asking, I said, "That's external. How about internal power?"

Many said they'd never been taught it. After ten minutes of this open Q&A conversation, it was becoming clear that none of those in my seminar had any idea where they got their power. Finally, in the deathly silence, one brave soul said, "I'm a sixth degree black belt, and I raised my hand because I was embarrassed not to, but the truth is I don't know."

I told him that he gave me the best, cleverest, and most beautiful answer of them all—that he didn't know. This is what I want to give people, these three things that most don't know: (1) where their power comes from, (2) how to access it, and (3) how to use it in a good way.

With six-time MMA World Champion Gokor Chivichyan, who has 10,000 students, handles 20 UFC fighters, and teaches seminars worldwide. I am proud to be teaching kickboxing at the Hayastan MMA Academy.

A year after the Jet's Gym closed, I began receiving messages from a man named Fariborz Azhakh, who owns a martial arts school in Woodland Hills. His calls came almost weekly and always with the same message—please call back regarding taking lessons. At some point, I became aware of his background. Fariborz held a 7th degree black belt in traditional hapkido under Master Sexton, whose name I had known for years. In addition to training with Master Sexton, Fariborz was active in tournament competition in the early1980s and performed in front of Mr. Parker in August 1989 at the 25th (Silver) anniversary of the Long Beach Internationals.

Finally after more than a year of these phone calls, I decided to pay him a visit, if for no other reason than I wanted to meet this guy who was so persistent. When one afternoon I appeared at his school unannounced, he was surprised. He was even more surprised when I refused to enter his school to talk with him, but instead told him we'd talk around the corner at a sandwich shop. I wanted to talk with him as a person, not as the head instructor of Team Karate Centers. When we arrived at the eatery, I didn't eat. When he asked why I wasn't eating, I told him that I didn't come to eat with him, and then flatly asked him what he wanted. I could tell that he wasn't used to someone like me being so direct. The main reason I had brought him to the lunch shop was because I wanted to observe how he ate, and I especially wanted to see how he interacted with the people who served him.

As it turned out, Fariborz's wife, Nina, had been studying kickboxing for a few years with my top student Peter "Sugarfoot" Cunningham. During a conversation Fariborz had with Cecile Peoples, Cecile suggested to Fariborz that he contact me to see if I would accept him as a student—thus the more than a year of weekly phone calls. Following our brief discussion at the sandwich shop, we returned to his school and he showed me around. The school was larger than most and clearly well organized.

My kickboxing ring at Team Karate Centers

After a few more weeks of discussion, I agreed to take Fariborz on as a student. Six months into our training, he one day said, "Sensei, this dojo is yours. Here's the key."

"Wait a minute," I replied. "How do you know if I even want to be here?"

"It's yours if you want it," he insisted. "I'd love to have you be a part of this. I'm not asking for anything, not even for you to affiliate your name with my school or to use you in any way to recruit students. Just consider this place your home. I'm just offering and not asking and not asking anything in return."

I had no doubt that he was totally sincere and that the unselfish offer he made came from his heart. I told him I'd think it over and left. Over the next two weeks, I returned to the school to observe his students and see how they acted with him. I talked privately with many of his black belts and even many of his lower belts, questioning how they felt about their instructor and the

school. Moreover, I talked with the business owners in the small shopping mall where the school is located.

Without exception, everyone I spoke with held Fariborz in great esteem and admiration and loved the dojo. Because I'd come to all the same conclusions, I accepted his offer to consider the Team Karate Centers my home base. In time, I established a small office at the school, and even erected my boxing ring and bags in a private area, along with all my championship belts.

FACING: Teaching at Team Karate Centers; BELOW: With Sensei Fariborz

With Majid Racees, one of my protégés

In addition to having a warm heart and gentle soul, Fariborz truly proved that he possesses the warrior's heart of a lion when one day he told me that on Jan 5, 2012, in celebration of his 50th birthday, he wanted to fight 50 rounds of sparring. To say that this was a monumental task would be a vast understatement. One by one—fighting with courage and veracity—he met all 50 opponents that included Steve Sexton, Dave Kovar, Ron Balicki, Cecil Peoples, Diana Lee Inosanto, Pete Cunningham, Ernie Reyes Jr., Simon Rhee, Nicolas Saignac. As an aside, I was his 50th opponent. Along with everyone else who was honored to have witnessed this remarkable feat, I was incredibly proud of him that day.

Congratulating Sensei Fariborz after his grueling 50 rounds of kickboxing

ABOVE: Kicking during my daily workout; BELOW: With Sara on our daily morning jog

ABOVE: With my daughter Monique; BELOW: Enjoying a great evening with friends and family on my 60th birthday

With Sara and Levi

ELEVEN

What the Future Holds

▼ ▼ ▼ ▼

B etween the ages of 14 and 21, I ruled the night, the witching hour, because I understood it so well. The underground world was about using the emotional trappings of anger, fear, frustration, and anxieties to shoot down people with those types of negative energies. Over many years, I consciously learned how to do that so that I could control most everyone around me in order to get what I wanted.

In looking back, I escaped death far too many times to have been coincidental. How did I survive all that craziness? Today I believe that Maker allowed me to move forward because He had a better plan for me that I couldn't see when I was living in darkness.

Perhaps Maker was telling me that the time had come for me to clean up my karma for all the damage I'd done. Maybe God's plan all along was to take me through all that darkness so that I could better understand people who live in the dark. Even if this were true, it was my decision, my ignorance, my stubbornness, and my blindness that allowed me to walk in darkness for all those years. I can't put that on Maker because I truly believe that God has always wanted only the best for me.

During my incarceration in the early 1970s, I began questioning why all this had happened to me. After I was released from prison and married Sara, I started traveling. Whenever Sara was with me, which was often, we visited churches and other sacred places and began questioning spiritually knowledgeable people we came upon. The early 1970s marked the beginning of my spiritual search.

It was around this time that Sara began bringing out her medicine (As a footnote, when I use the word medicine, I'm referring to teachings and ancient practices that a healer uses to physically, mentally, and emotionally help a person heal). After following Sara's medicine for a while, I started bringing forth my own medicine. Within a few months, we both became so excited and absorbed with our medicines that we began seeking out the medicines of different countries. After a year, my medicine began to fully develop, so much so that there was no question in my mind—I knew I had it.

Although I had become intimately familiar with my medicine, I didn't yet know how to use it until I started working with other masters, who started weaning me and feeding me. The more I worked with these ancient healers, the more came out of me. At one point, I found myself wondering where did all this come from. No one had taught me this medicine, and I knew I hadn't read it anywhere. After considerable reflection, it suddenly dawned on me that I'd come into the world with it.

Throughout the 1980s, I was no longer in the dark and was walking in the light. Because of this, I was able to acquire a full understanding of my medicine and my gifts, which further encouraged Sara and me to continue seeking out other people in the light and sharing our light with one another. To date, this had been the greatest period of spiritual growth in my life.

By the end of the 1980s, I was healing people. I was so enthralled by this gift that now and then I found myself thinking, how did I do that? and how did I know that? Did I do this before? And then again I would remember, I did do this. I was here. I did have this medicine. Realizing that I could be a healer was a great revelation—to suddenly know that I could do something good and to finally be able to clearly identify what would become my most important life's work.

A key aspect of my spiritual growth that came to me near the end of the 1980s was my need to establish a happy medium between all that is present in both the darkness and the light. I often refer to this as balance, and it is critical to everything in life. Everything must be in moderation. For example, too much love becomes unhealthy because it changes to need—I want more, I have to have more. When healthy love becomes unbalanced, it turns to addiction. Not enough love, and the person feels they're not good enough and are undeserving of the other person.

Balance in everything, no matter what it is. Too much of vitamins is unhealthy; not enough vitamins is unhealthy. Too much food is not good, not enough food is not good. Too much water is not good, not enough water is not good. Most important of all is to maintain a balance between the dark and the light and to respect both.

Maintaining a balance in all aspects of my life was the key to keeping my life running smoothly. This is similar to an airplane that continues in flight by keeping several opposing forces in balance. Gravity wants to bring the plane to the ground while the plane's jet engines continually work against gravity by lifting the aircraft. This balance of the two opposing forces—along with balancing the aircraft's pitch, yaw, and roll axes—is what keeps a massive aircraft steadily moving forward in a smooth, straight line. It's a highly delicate formula. One uncorrected mistake in balance and the aircraft will fall to the ground.

Because of many spiritual experiences, I'm convinced beyond a shadow of a doubt that I've lived previous lives as a warrior, be it a gladiator, a samurai, and even a ninja. As a result, I came into this world with profound knowledge of warfare that included an understanding of mental warfare, physical warfare, spiritual warfare, and character warfare.

With regard to the samurai, to be an effective leader, a samurai needed to be familiar with many professions and all types of people. Most important, he had to know his own body better than anyone else did because he often had to prevent and treat his own illnesses and injuries. In essence, he was an educated healer who took good care of his own body, trained with regular exercise in addition to practicing the combat arts, and was a primitive expert on nutrition. Moreover, in addition to being a physical warrior, the samurai was a master in self-knowledge, overcoming self-deception in order to see himself, other people, the world, and a higher power more clearly.

In my opinion, a true warrior of today who lives the Way of Bushido must be, like the samurai, a master of life strategies. He's a combination teacher, martial artist focused on reality-based self-defense, scholar, role model, and healer of physical, mental, emotional, and spiritual pain and suffering.

I fought because I could, but fighting isn't what I came here for. I came here to teach—not to teach people how to live their lives, but a way of life. Due to my many years of teaching internal martial arts training, people are coming to me because they now want to go inside. Most have the outside. Physical training is an external thing. You kick. You punch. You stretch. You work on endurance. Most proficient martial artists now understand that the internal is far more important.

I believe 80% of success is mental. Only 20% is physical, but 99.99999% is also emotional. The moment you allow your emotions to enter into your 80% mental, you'll start to get results you're NOT looking for. Or you'll be creating results that you ARE looking for—one or the other. The choice is yours.

I'm not about an idea. I'm about the solution to getting unstuck. I like to teach people how their voice can be healing and comforting and how their demeanor of energy can be of service to others—that's internal. This is what people are searching for, to understand the purpose and reason why they exist.

If I want to be used as an instrument for a higher source, I need to access the darkness in order to help people in need. If I want to be used as a spirit of Maker's love in order to help people, I have to be in the midst of the sorrow, pain, confusion, and the decay. I need to go to purgatory and gather their souls so that they can be reborn.

When a person pulls themselves from the darkness, they do so both physically and spiritually. When they leave this dark place, it's vital that they travel to a calm place where they are able to physically and spiritually channel energy. This place of calm is what I refer to as a "safe haven" and is where people can see their gifts that they came into the world with.

I am presently in the planning stage of opening an internal school, which will serve as a safe haven. Along with Sara, I'm going to have many Native American chiefs and elders from different tribes. I have permission from the Blackfoot Nation to build this safe haven that was designed by Willy Big Bull. Among other things, this place will include an indoor sweat lodge, which has never been done. In this safe haven, there's going to be physical warfare, mental warfare, spiritual warfare, and character warfare. This will be a place where people can come and find their truth and learn about themselves by going back to the mother's womb, which means starting again from the beginning. In many ways this safe haven will function as a school and will contain everything from anger management to college courses to learning to identify one's gifts and how to bring them forward.

My Native American ways that were taught to me by my mother, as well as the ways that were taught to Sara by her Uncle Domingo, will be a major part of the foundation of this safe haven. For example, in our ways, we believe in the spirit of Great Spirit and Mother Earth and that everything has energy and is alive. Bringing the Native American ways forward to where we return to the mother womb to the beginning is what facilitates full understanding. It's about going back to the purity of who you are. In common day computer jargon, this process is identical to pressing the reset button and rebooting our computer to all of its default settings. When this process occurs to a person, they're no longer blocked by the negative emotions of anger, fear, frustration, anxiety, and sadness, but instead are open to view something that is naturally beautiful. Nature is as natural as it can be.

Of course, the martial arts will be a part of this safe haven because my entire life has been rooted in the martial arts, which includes Indian warfare and Indian wild fighting. At this safe haven, I intend to restore much of the Bushido Way to the martial arts. Decades ago, we came with honor, but unfortunately have lost much of it along the way.

Some of what I teach of the internal was tested on the Breakfast Club because the Breakfast Club was a metaphor of the square jungle, which includes a person's home, work, and the people around them. The square jungle will bring forward one's truth, as well as all the negative emotions that an individual hides inside. Once exposed, my job is to reprogram that person. If a person doesn't like the way they feel, I help them change the way they think. In a sense, I'm a reprogrammer.

The world we live in has radically changed over the past 25 years. Because we place such a heavy reliance on computer technology, our senses have become dulled. We don't see as well as we used to. Our hearing and sense of smell have been diminished, as well as our innate powers of instinct and intuition.

Because our outer and inner senses have been bombarded by radio waves, television waves, satellite signals, X-rays, gamma rays, cellphone transmissions, and so forth, our world has become so loud and tasteless that we question everything that arrives through our senses. As you walk along a busy street in a major city, the energy from all the people around you, as well as all the invisible signals and wavelengths, are bouncing off the walls. You get a sudden thought and wonder why am I thinking this? Although the thought process is in your head, it's not necessarily yours. Instead, you're picking things up from other originating sources. This is why traveling to a safe haven where everything is quiet and still is vital to your getting back in touch with your center by returning to your beginnings. You need to be in a calm place so that you can hear.

Besides becoming loud, our world has become a lonely place. What was once a personal world has become painfully impersonal. People feel insignificant because our computerized world has resulted in less personal attention to our needs. We don't need to have great memories because we have 10 gigabytes of memory on our smart phones. We don't need to remember anything, not even where we live because our car's GPS will get us home. We don't need to calculate anything because everything from balancing our checkbook to leaving the correct tip in a restaurant can be done through our cellphone. We don't need to spend quality time finding a mate. All we need do is log onto many of the Internet matchmaking websites. On a much broader scale, our instant access to knowledge via Internet search engines is boundless.

For members of our younger generations, this problem is compounded because while they have all this technology at their fingertips, they have no experience behind this knowledge. In a sense, they live in a virtual world. They know, they know, they know, but yet they know very little because they have no real time experience.

I'm especially motivated when working with the young generations because many of them are so confused about what it takes to survive in this day and age. Many of them don't understand why they're here. Often I'll hear them say, "I didn't ask to be born. And if I did ask to be born, I would've asked to be born to parents who are wealthy so I didn't have to grow up poor and be hungry half the time." Other questions that I often hear are, "Why is my life like this?" "Why am I so sad?" "Why am I so angry in life?" "Why do I hate myself?" and "Why do I think I don't deserve anything?" This generation is caught up in a whirlwind of emotion, and they don't know how to get out.

Many of the people I work with come to me because they're wanting peace of mind. They want to know why they're here on Earth. They want to uncover their gifts and learn how to use them. After working with me for a short time, they come to recognize that everything they're searching for they already brought with them into this world. The key in discovering these gifts is to "forget what they know and remember what they forgot."

Let me give you an example of what I mean by that. Whether you knew it or not, you were born into this world with the full knowledge of knowing how to swim and swim well. We know this because young babies can be pulled underwater by their mothers, and these babies will instinctively hold their breath and swim a short distance to another person. And they do this with a smile on their face and without fear. The majority of babies, however, aren't subjected to this peaceful expression of their natural swimming ability. Instead, their parents soon program their young children to avoid going near the water because the water is a potentially dangerous place that could result in drowning. As a result, these children forget their innate swimming ability and develop a fear of the water. It is no surprise that years later their parents are forced to enroll their children in swimming lessons so that their kids can learn how to swim. So by "forget what you know and remember what you forgot" means to forget the fear that your parents instilled in you about large bodies of water and simply remember your innate ability to swim.

Another example is fighting. Like all children, I was born with the knowledge of fighting, no different from a lion cub that instinctively knows how to protect itself when it leaves the protection of its mother. Although the great majority of parents discourage their child's aggressive behavior, and in fact program such aggressiveness out of them, my father didn't do this. Quite the contrary, my dad encouraged my fighting at an early age. In addition, he didn't instill fear in me. As a result, I never forgot my instinctive ability to fight because it was never programmed out of me. I didn't have to "remember what I forgot." What I came in with I embraced throughout my fight career and became a champion. No martial arts teacher anywhere can teach me to protect my physical well-being better than Maker can.

The process of forgetting what we know is programmed in us by our first teachers—our parents. They're the ones who are closest to us and the ones who program us with their fear, frustration, anger, and anxiety. They do this not out of spite, but because they're trying to protect us. They want us to be fearful of strangers, fire, large bodies of water—and taking risks—for good reason. They're doing their jobs by tilting the playing field in their child's favor. But there's a heavy price for this. Often it's the loss of a child's gifts and their knowing why they were sent into this world. They grow up as adults not knowing who they really are. And in most cases they're right. The end result is that what they've done in life is what they were programmed to be, but that's not who they are.

One and two year old toddlers look into the air and talk to somebody. Babies have acute senses and perceptions that allow them to see things that their parents don't. Their parents put things into their child's playpen fully believing that these things are what their child wants and needs. The child has no idea about all this stuff and doesn't care because it's playing with the quilt. This programing that parents do begins from the moment of birth and in many cases continues well into adulthood; hence the frustrated adult who sighs, "I'm tired of trying to live up to my parents' expectations."

People who come to my safe haven need not train in the martial arts—all can come. From five years of age, with few exceptions, everyone is taken through the process of remembering everything they forgot, which essentially is their innate brilliance. Forget what you know and remember what you forgot is a three-fold process of uncover, discover, and discard. The result is that the person uncovers and discovers their gifts, and then discards all that they learned that works against the fulfillment of their purpose in life.

I'm a teacher because I'm teaching people about themselves. I'm teaching them how to excel and stay in that feeling, as well as teaching them what not to do in life. Looking at the big picture, I teach people the inner, the outer, and the middle ways of fulfilling everything in life they were brought here to fulfill. In reprogramming people, I heal their mind. I'm a troubleshooter who throws a lifeline to a person who is trapped in quicksand, knowing that the more they struggle, the faster they will go under. Rescuing them from purgatory and taking them to a safe haven is the first step in helping them get their life on track.

Since making the decision to not control me or anything around me, great things began happening in my life. By committing myself to allowing God use me as an instrument of His love, I've been able to see where previously I was blind.

I came into this world as a teacher. I love teaching. I love helping someone become a better person. I knew nothing of that part of me until 21 years of age. I didn't know something real like that could be possible in my life because I was living with so much inner turmoil. Truly, today I'm finally balanced. I'm happy that I can see clearly. I learned to heal all of my tikkuns that I brought with me into this world, and over time learned to heal all the wounds of my body (Tikkun is a Hebrew word that means "repairing or healing the world." The word world applies to one's personal world as well as all of humanity). Today I'm grateful to be a servant of a higher service of God and help people mentally, physically, and spiritually. Today I truly understand my purpose in life and why I exist.

I've lived many previous lives, and it has taken me many centuries to get to this point of understanding of where I am today. Even though I'm an old soul, in my present life, I'm enjoying living one day at a time being a servant of a higher source.

I think people will remember me as a teacher; not as a coach, not as a trainer, but as a teacher. To this day, I've always thought I was a better teacher than a fighter. I don't want to be remembered for what I DID. I want to be remembered for who I AM. I came into this world as a teacher. I want to leave this world as a teacher.

When my eyes open in the morning, my first words are THANK YOU. Thank you that I have another day to be with people who I truly love, particularly Sara. No matter where I went throughout my fight career, she was present with my mother, my sisters, and my brothers. She was my biggest fan. After my mother passed, Sara took the place of my mother in a spiritual realm of power and strength, but she also stood as my lover, the mother of my child, and my partner. As I did with my mother, I can rest my head on Sara's lap and feel safe. She can tap her knee and I can go to her and close my eyes and be at peace. My wife, who is also my best friend, is a major part of my life and my safe haven.

I don't take a single day for granted. I ask Maker for the courage to do something that I couldn't do yesterday. If it's asking for forgiveness or giving forgiveness, so be it, but to have the courage to do it—today. Then I ask for sight that I may see my gifts because if I ask for help and I can't see it—if help comes my way and passes me—that would be a tragedy. When I ask for help and it comes my way, then I can receive the blessings so that I can move forward. Most of all, I want my words to be impeccable. I don't talk just to talk or hurt people with my words. I ask that I may use my words in a wise way that I may make sense to people in a way that might help them on their journey. That's what I want people to reflect upon when they think about The Jet.

Benny "The Jet" Urquidez
Kenpo Shotokan Black Belts

1st Degree

Mike Avila
Tom Blaswick
Tony Campos
Louie Cercedes
Sonny Covarrubias
Denise Doe Shea
Debbie Doucette
Hank Garrett

Manuel Hernandez
Johnny Martinez
Joe Montero
Mark Parra
John Spencer
Sara Urquidez
Armando Urquidez

2nd Degree

Freddy Aviles

4th Degree

Alfred Urquidez

5th Degree

Blinky Rodriguez
Adam (Smiley) Urquidez

Lilly Urquidez Rodriguez
Michael White

10th Degree

Arnold Urquidez
Benny Urquidez

Ruben Urquidez

Benny "The Jet" Urquidez Kickboxing Instructors

Level 5

Fariborz Azhakh
Louie Cercedes
Glen Coxin
Angel Delamora
Matt Fleuret
Gino Frazier
Raymond Garcia
Manuel Hernandez
Johnny Martinez

Rick Monahan
Michael Morteo
Mark Parra
Steve Shauger
Monique Urquidez
Carol Urquidez
Linda Vogel
Harry Zegel

Level 6

Gloria Alvarado
Rick Anderson
Freddy Aviles
Abe Belardo
Scott Bernstein
Nadine Champion
John Cusack
Cody Davis
Alex Desir
Jimmy Fishman
Hank Garrett
John Hackleman
Vince Imbornone
Dale Jacoby
Ken Lally
Damon Levy
Stan Longinidis
Jimmy Lui
Duff McKaggen

Rick Mendiola
Jim Murphy
Pierre Narvades
Richard Norton
Ricky OKane
Patrick Outlaw
Hector Pena
Nelson Plasencia
Bridgette Riley
Robert Rodriguez
John Spencer
Danny Steel
Aaron Tavdi
Alfred Urquidez
Sara Urquidez
Melvin Wells
Michael White
Walt Woodsen
Greg Yates

Level 7

Peter Cunningham
Jeff Mulvin
Majid Raees

- Thunderwolf
AJ Urquidez

Level 8

Blinky Rodriguez
Adam (Smiley) Urquidez

Lilly Urquidez Rodriguez

Level 9

Arnold Urquidez
Benny Urquidez

Ruben Urquidez

Benny "The Jet" Urquidez Ukidokan Karate Black Belt

1st Degree Black Belt

Tom Blaswick
Louie Cercedes
Nadine Champion
Sonny Covarrubias
Glen Coxin
Peter Cunningham
Angel Delamora
Alex Desir
Gino Frazier
Manuel Hernandez
Johnny Martinez
Joe Montero
Jeff Mulvin

Dave Mustaine
Ricky OKane
Mark Parra
Majid Raees
Robert Rodriguez
John Spencer
- Thunderwolf
AJ Urquidez
Monique Urquidez
Sara Urquidez
Melvin Wells
Harry Zegel

2nd Degree Black Belt

Tony Campos

3rd Degree Black Belt

Delores Urquidez

4th Degree Black Belt

Abe Belardo
Alfred Urquidez
Lilly Urquidez Rodriguez

5th Degree Black Belt

Blinky Rodriguez
Adam (Smiley) Urquidez
Michael White

7th Degree Black Belt

Armando Urquidez
Ruben Urquidez

9th Degree Black Belt

Benny Urquidez

People who have influenced my martial arts

Muhammad Ali

Ralph Castro

Gokor Chivichyan

Al Dacascos

Dan Inosanto

Takayuki Kubota

Tom LaPuppet

Gene LeBell

Bruce Lee

Steve Muhammad

Chuck Norris

Masutatsu Oyama

Ed Parker

Bill Ryusaki

Mike Stone

Arnold Urquidez

Lilly Urquidez Rodriguez

Douglas Wong

Tadashi Yamashita

About the Authors

▼ ▼ ▼ ▼

Proclaimed by many of the great masters of our time to be the greatest pound-for-pound kickboxer of all time, Benny Urquidez was nicknamed "The Jet" because of his explosive spinning back kick. After competing for ten years in non-contact point karate, he pioneered full-contact fighting throughout the world, often fighting in bouts where the rules were ambiguous and contrasts in styles were dramatic.

In the 1970s, he won the PKA and WKA World Kickboxing Championships, and then went on to defeat Japan's World Champion. Highlighting his stellar career that spanned two decades, Urquidez came out of semi-retirement at the age of 42 to seal his legendary status by defeating Japan's 25-year-old reigning World Champion. Victorious in six World Championships in five different weight divisions, Benny "The Jet" Urquidez has remained undefeated for 27 years as the longest reigning World Champion ever.

Unofficially retired from professional kickboxing in 1995, Sensei Benny Urquidez continues to teach martial arts at the Team Karate Centers in Woodland Hills, California, regularly works in the Hollywood film industry as an actor and fight choreographer, and travels the world with his wife Sara Eaglewoman as a spiritual teacher.

Tom Bleecker began his writing career in 1969 as a screenwriter for director Blake Edwards. After nearly two decades writing for screen and television, in 1987 Bleecker co-authored his first book with Linda Lee, *The Bruce Lee Story*, which served as the source material for MCA Universal's motion picture *Dragon*. In 1996, Bleecker wrote a second book on Lee, a highly controversial bestseller entitled *Unsettled Matters*. After penning nearly 50 biographies, in 2012 Bleecker wrote his first novel *Tea Money*. The author and his wife, Lourdes, live in Southern California.

Gene LeBell is an American martial artist, instructor, stunt performer, and professional wrestler. Labeled as "The Toughest Man Alive" by many martial arts masters, Gene LeBell has worked on more than 1,000 films and television shows and has authored a number of books. He lives in Los Angeles with his wife, Midge.

"Benny Urquidez is a true martial arts warrior. He is not only an exceptional martial artist but he has the biggest and kindest heart of anyone I've met. It is a blessing to have Benny as a friend. We love you Benny!"

—*Cynthia Rothrock*

"In my estimation, Benny is probably the best fighter to have come from the United States, maybe even the entire world. He fought under all rules and was fearless in his movement. He is a great friend and I cherish his friendship and am very jealous of his abilities."

—*Superfoot Bill Wallace*

"I consider Sensei Benny Urquidez an icon in the martial arts world and a true warrior in the ring! He is a compassionate and patient teacher of fundamentals on the mat and a humble gentleman off the mat."

—*Mike Swain, 4 x Judo Olympian*

"Benny 'The Jet' was always a gentleman with a fighter's heart. During the time of full contact fighting, he was the name that drew in the crowd. Pound for pound he's a proven champion inside and out. When you hear his name, no matter where in the world you are, it is the one and only 'Benny the Jet.'"

—*Al Dacascos*

"I have been fortunate enough to have become friends with my teacher who will always remain a master. His story captivates as much as it inspires. Lightning speed and fierce grace in the ring made him a legend; but his kindness and generosity in his life are what I most admire about him. Sensei Benny is the ideal balance of character and expertise."

—Sensei Fariborz

"Benny Urquidez is the greatest full contact karate fighter in martial arts history. He kept the art alive for decades and paved the way for today's mixed martial arts fighters. His pioneering accomplishments make him one of the most historic figures of our generation."

—Michael Matsuda,
President Martial Arts History Museum

"Back in the 1970s, I read about the exploits of Sensei Benny Urquidez when professional martial arts fighting was growing, when contests and rules were in an experimental stage. Benny 'The Jet' has secured a well-earned reputation as one of the greatest kickboxers of all time."

—Stephen Quadros, "The Fight Professor"

"Sensei Benny Urquidez is a gentleman and a true martial artist. His strength lies in his humility and his willingness to share his knowledge with others, regardless of style or creed. Sensei Benny will remain as one of the greatest fighter and contributors to the martial arts world."

—Phillip Rhee

"Benny Urquidez had no peers in the early days of world class kickboxing. He personified for me the best of what martial arts stars should be—deadly, humble, and inspiring."

—*Joe Corley, CEO PKA Warriors*

"Benny 'The Jet' was a champion in point fight tournaments, but when he transitioned to full contact karate, he became a super champion and the first martial arts fighter to be an international celebrity."

—*Pat Worley*

"Master Benny has deeply inspired me. Many professional fighters become and stay fighters, but Master Benny has evolved into a master teacher of the physical and spiritual aspects of the martial arts."

—*Tom Callos*

"Benny Urquidez is arguably the most famous full contact fighter who ever lived. The martial arts world would not be where it is today had there never been Benny 'The Jet' Urquidez. I am proud to say that he is a friend."

—*Steve Sexton*

"Sensei Benny 'The Jet' Urquidez is a teacher, philosopher, warrior, champion, and role model. I am honored to have trained and studied under both him and his legendary brothers and sister, Lilly."

—*Peter "Sugarfoot" Cunningham*

"Benny is proof positive that the wisdom of Solomon and the skills of the greatest warriors of the ages can be reincarnated into one person. There will never be another warrior the likes of Benny The Jet."

—Gregory Yates, long time student

"In the United States, the martial arts industry began with a small group of legends and superstars. Some produced phenomenal students; some wound up in the motion picture industry; some created large systems; and some became legendary world-class fighters. Mr. Urquidez has accomplished all of these things."

—Ed Parker, Jr., Paxtial Arts Founder

"In my 50 years in the martial arts, I have met and competed against some of the world's finest martial artists. Benny Urquidez stands alone. Many fighters brag about their victories, but Benny Urquidez is so well respected that people brag about being in the ring with him, and being defeated by him. He is a legend. He exemplifies class and the warrior spirit, and I am proud to call him my friend."

—Bob White